Jasmin Yildiz

I WASN'T TOLD THE HALF OF IT

The Queen of Sheba's journey

to visit King Solomon

Foreword and postscript by Werner Gitt

Homepage of Dr. Werner Gitt: www.wernergitt.de

Here you can find:
- List of current lecture dates
- Essays and books in various languages for downloading
- Tracts (e.g. 'How can I get to Heaven?', 'Who is the Designer?', 'Miracles in the Bible', 'What Darwin couldn't know', '…and He DOES exist!', 'Crib, Cross and Crown', 'One-way Journey', 'The Greatest Invitation') for downloading in over 65 languages.

Homepage of the Illustrator Doris Daubertshäuser: www.doris-made-to-create.de

Jasmin Yildiz
I wasn't told the half of it
The Queen of Sheba's journey to visit King Solomon
Foreword and epilogue by Werner Gitt

First Edition 2015
© Lichtzeichen Verlag/Publishers, Lage, Germany
Original Title: Nicht die Hälfte hat man mir gesagt
– Die Reise der Königin von Saba zu König Salomo
Editor of German original: Werner Gitt
Illustrations: Doris Dauberthäuser
Translation from the German: Brigitte Stoll,
Dr Carl Wieland
ISBN: 978-3-86954-189-1 (Englisch/English)
Order-No. 548189

Contents

Foreword..5

The Queen of Sheba's journey—from a historical
perspective 11

The biblical text relating to the Queen of Sheba's
journey 115

The only life-story in world history that was ever
foretold..117

Epilogue—part I: Retrospective..................135

Epilogue—part II: The Queen of Sheba's journey—
from a New Testament perspective 137

Epilogue—part III: How can I get to Heaven?.........163

Foreword

Many places in the Bible recount conversations that God Himself, His angels or His prophets had with mortal men. In the New Testament, we read of Jesus and His apostles speaking with their contemporaries. In all these conversations, only the essential elements or the outcomes have been recorded in the Bible.

Thus, the lengthy night-time discourse between Jesus and Nicodemus (John 3:1–11) is recounted in only eleven verses. And of the conversation leading to Matthew's conversion, only one single verse is recorded for us (Matthew 9:9). We can, however, assume that Jesus engaged with all the questions put to Him by any seeker. His apostles acted similarly, as did Old Testament characters.

If everything had been written down which even Jesus alone said and did, all the world's books would not be sufficient to record it (John 21:25). Because the biblical accounts of events and conversations have mostly been kept very short, there is ample 'room to move' when developing sermon material.

A good sermon should not be a mere recital of a biblical story; rather, it should give form to the story and illuminate it. This is often best done via a free-flowing retelling of the text in question—as well as using conclusions from the text, and complementary proof texts from the rest of Scripture, to expound the passage. And, especially, to point to Christ the Saviour.

This same leeway is also available to us in making the accounts relevant to today's audiences through retelling in a free narrative style, as well as supplementing details from the historical context which are helpful to understanding the divine message. All this, however, must be so constructed as not to contradict the overarching testimony of the Bible.

The New Testament (Acts 8:26–40) contains the interesting story of the Treasurer of Ethiopia, which is particularly well-suited to explain the Gospel to people who have never yet heard it. Since this heathen Ethiopian had not heard anything of the good news of Jesus, Philip had to explain it to him in detail, as if in a beginner's course of the faith.

Jasmin Yildiz, in the well-presented paperback 'No Journey Too Far', has re-created the lead-up to the encounter between the Treasurer and Philip in detail and with narrative licence. She describes his stay in Jerusalem as it might very likely have played out, constructing several conversations with both religious and unbelieving citizens of Jerusalem. These are intended to show that the Treasurer was unable to find an answer there to his search for God. That only happened in his conversation with Philip in the desert.

There is a second fascinating story in the Bible that has particularly resonated with me. It is the Old Testament (OT) account of the Queen of Sheba's journey to the wise King Solomon of Israel. During ministry trips both in Germany and abroad it has given me much joy to preach repeatedly on the text from 2 Chronicles 9:1–12. I approach it from the New Testament perspective, in line with the principle of interpretation given by Jesus: "You search the Scriptures because you think that in them you have eternal life; and it is they that bear witness about me" (John 5:39). That sermon is reproduced in the Appendix.

In response to an enquiry from the Lichtzeichen Publishers for another evangelistic book similar to the story of the Treasurer, it seemed obvious that *Jasmin Yildiz* should be asked to flesh out the remarkable account of the Queen of Sheba in the same way she has already done with the journey of the Ethiopian Treasurer. This book is the outcome. As well as being interesting, the narrative is also very instructive, as it deals with the core teachings of the Old Testament in dialogue form. The aim of the book was not to produce an entertaining novel, but rather to bring these central OT themes to life, using the technique of a dialogue over several days between Solomon and the Sheban queen.

The queen came from a pagan land where there was no knowledge of the living God; so, she is the ideal person to ask Solomon all those questions about God and the world which also exercise our thinking in the 21st century.

Solomon was gifted by God with exceptional wisdom; so, he is also the right person to answer all these questions in the light of God's Word.

With empathy and insight, *Jasmin Yildiz* has managed to appropriately portray this queen with her alert, inquiring mind, who repeatedly challenges Solomon with pointed questions. In her treatment of the material, the author has, out of a multitude of Old Testament prophecies, particularly prioritized those dealing with the Messiah.

So as not to be hampered by the omission of certain essential prophetic utterances in the Old Testament which were only given in the period *after* Solomon (e.g. Isaiah, Daniel and Zechariah) she took the poetic licence to include these as well. In the chapter following the story she demonstrates that all prophecies concerning the Messiah have been completely fulfilled in Jesus.

From these interestingly depicted conversations between the king and the queen we can learn much:

There is only one true God, namely the God of the Bible.

No god of the nations has ever directly revealed Himself to human beings. All such gods thereby declare themselves null and void, because none but the God of the Bible has directly revealed Himself to humans.

The prophetic utterances pointing to the Messiah and their fulfilment in Jesus prove the Bible to be the sole divine source of information.

God's love and compassion is available for people of every nation.

This God of the Bible can be found by anyone who seeks Him with a sincere heart.

In the epilogue it will then be demonstrated, step by step, how the reader may personally come to faith.

I would like to thank my faithful colleague *Doris Daubertshaeuser* who has created all the illustrations. *Gerhard Cumme* and *Christian Leonhartsberger* have previously read and critiqued the manuscript of the book and I am most grateful for all pointers and suggestions for improvement.

I am also very grateful to the Lichtzeichen Verlag (Publishing House), particularly *Thomas Schneider* and *Michael Baehr* for their helpful collaboration in the publishing and formation of this book. Also to *Brigitte Stoll* and her brother *Carl Wieland* for translation into English from the original German.

Werner Gitt

The Queen of Sheba's Journey—from a historical perspective

Childhood

An old lady with grey hair and deep furrows in her face sat on the sofa and told a story. Beside her lay a little girl with legs stretched out, listening intently. The girl's long, chestnut-brown hair hung down a long way over her shoulders. Her chin resting on her hands, she watched every movement of the old lady, who continued her story:

"Then God stroked the cheek of the child to comfort it and said it should not be sad that it was going to die shortly. 'It is my gift to you, my child, so that you do not have to suffer long in this world!' God comforted the child."

The little girl interrupted the old lady, who was such a good story-teller: "But grandmother, how does God know when the child will die?" The grandmother looked sternly at the girl, as if wanting to know whether she wanted to hear exciting stories or ask questions. "Just let me finish, will you?" responded the old lady.

"But grandmother, I want to know how come God knows it!"

"Because God knows everything", suggested the grandmother.

"Which god is it then, who is all-knowing?"

"The god of heaven."

"So, whose god is He then?" the girl continued to question.

"He is one of the gods of the Sabeans," the old lady added.

"But from where does this god of heaven get His ability to know everything? I don't understand this", the girl persisted.

Her grandmother gently stroked the girl's chestnut-brown head and added: "Because He made us, He has to be all-knowing.[1] Where His all-encompassing knowledge comes from, we don't know."

"If He is all-knowing, why then did He make my little brother blind and deaf? Perhaps the god of the Sabeans was not all-knowing after all", the girl remarked shrewdly.

"You're right, my child! The god of heaven has made some of us healthy and others deaf and blind. Why he has so determined it, we do not know, because he has not revealed himself." Then the grandmother asked the girl if she wanted to hear how the story continued.

---

[1] With the help of 'Natural Laws of Information' it can be shown that the Originator of information in living creatures has to be all-knowing. See W. Gitt *et. al.*, *Without Excuse*, Creation Book Publishers, Powder Springs, GA, 2011.

Probing questions

"Most of all I'd like to know from where the god of heaven got this total knowledge, and why he didn't give it to us, too" the girl said sadly. "I always have to ask my teacher, because there are many things I don't understand. Couldn't the gods of the Sabeans have been generous and given their ability to know everything to us also, so that I can understand everything in school? Take my teacher; he torments me with his knowledge, because I don't understand it. You tell me stories about a god who comforts a little child because it will soon die, but he doesn't disclose *why* the child has to die at a young age."

This time the old lady stroked the soft skin of the girl's cheeks with her wrinkled hands as she sought to calm her: "We don't know this, my child! But perhaps a day will come when we do find out."

"I want to know it now!" the girl burst out, as if she had no time for the enigmatic nature of the god of the Sabeans.

"Just listen, my child, to what the god of the Sabeans said to the sick child!"

The girl did not seem eager to hear how the story continued. Instead she insisted that her grandmother explain to her why the god of the Sabeans kept his knowledge of everything hidden, like a buried treasure, so that the people he had created puzzled over it. Her

The young future Queen of Sheba loves to listen to her grand-mother's stories and asks her many questions.

grandmother realized that she did not need to continue with her stories, because the little girl was thirsty for the secrets of the divine.

After a short pause, the old lady finally said: "I, too, would love to know why the god of the Sabeans takes so much pleasure in being secretive. Unfortunately, the gods in Sheba don't disclose to us why one person has a long and merry life of revelry, while another has to endure a life of pain and suffering, until death finally releases him. Perhaps you will find out sometime, my child, because you have an insatiable thirst for knowledge. May the gods of the Sabeans one day reveal to you why they act as they do."

"Are the gods of the other nations also so secretive in their behaviour?" asked the girl.

"I don't know, but our gods haven't told us their secrets. Perhaps one day they might yet do so."

"Have they said when that will be?" The questions bubbled afresh out of the spirited girl.

"The gods of the Sabeans haven't spoken a single word to us. That's why we pray, so that they will speak to us. Perhaps they're angry with us, and that's why we give them all these offerings, so that they will be favourably disposed towards us."

"How do the people know that they are angry with us, when you say that they haven't spoken a word with any one of you? Perhaps they are neither kind nor angry?" the girl continued to ask in her curiosity.

The old lady was amazed at the girl's persistent questioning. "But we feel sure they must be angry with us."

"But perhaps they don't even exist, since they've spoken neither kind nor angry words with you", the girl proposed.

"Because the god of thunder sends us hail from heaven and so destroys our harvest, he must be angry with us!" her grandmother suggested anew.

"Did the gods of the Sabeans say that they are the cause of the hail pelting down from heaven?" her granddaughter asked, as though finally losing patience.

"Grandmother!" she burst out in agitation, "You believe in gods you don't even know; I can't believe in such gods."

"But we have believed in the gods of the Sabeans for generations!" she answered.

"Grandmother, have you at least met one of these gods of the Sabeans?"

"No!" answered the old lady. "So far, no-one has ever seen one of them."

"Why do the gods of the Sabeans hide themselves? Are they perhaps ugly, or sick? Perhaps they are all dead, grandmother?"

The old lady looked at the child in fear. "Child, you must not anger the gods of the Sabeans, or they will send us another drought!"

"But grandmother, think about what you're saying! You say that no-one has seen the gods of the Sabeans. They have spoken to no-one, nor have they sent anyone as a messenger, so that we will believe that they exist. See, my father receives ambassadors from every imaginable land, who represent the kings of their respective countries. Why don't the gods ever send an ambassador, if they are so powerful? These gods should at least be able to say: 'Hello, dear Sabeans, I am the god of heaven, or the thunder god of the Sabeans', so that you know with whom you're dealing!"

"What a sharp thinker you are, my child! Now I'm having to ask myself, too, why they don't do this."

"Grandmother, I would really like to have at least one single god show himself to me, so that I can trust him! If there even is such a thing as a god, I don't even know whether there is only one god, or two or three, or even many gods."

"But child, one day, when your father dies, you will be queen of this land of Sheba. You will need to keep your people united, and part of that is also our traditional belief in the gods. It is unthinkable that our queen should not believe in the gods of the Sabeans."

"But grandmother, how can I believe in gods that are invisible, or others that stand there before me, made of stone, like a monument, but cannot speak? I don't understand. How can I believe what I don't understand?"

The old lady could well understand the girl's rebellion against the gods. She had felt the same in her youth. At that time she had also asked herself, why most of the gods were enthroned on a high mountain and spoke not one word with mankind. Those gods that were visible, carved out of wood by humans, or chiselled out of stone, were so stone-dead that they couldn't utter even a single word. The others were invisible, and they, too, did not communicate with humans in any way. But over the years the old lady had come to terms with the fact that these gods were dead and silent.

These story-telling occasions between the grandmother and the little girl with the chestnut-brown hair continued over the following months and years. As the girl grew older, the conversations about the gods of the Sabeans became ever more lively. Her mental acumen sometimes proved too much for the old lady's ability to explain.

"Grandmother, what do you think, why do we have to make sacrifices to the gods?" the girl burst out one evening, as they were once again seated together comfortably. "I have heard that some families even offer their own children to the gods. Isn't that terrible?" Furrows appeared on the grandmother's forehead, as though she did not know what to say to her granddaughter. After a brief silence she suggested that it would appease one's conscience if one were to sacrifice one's dearest possession to the gods.

At this, the girl rebelled, just as young people today might react: "But grandmother, what sort of evil conscience it must be, that is only eased by killing innocent souls for it? One day, when I am Queen of Sheba, I intend to break with such traditions! I am only prepared to give everything precious I possess to the kind of god who shows himself to me, or sends his messenger.

"And while we're at it, grandmother, there's another question that bothers me: you had a mother, too—my great-grandmother. And your grandmother in turn had a mother, who then also had one. Did this go on like that into the past, back into endless eternity, or was there once a beginning?"

"Oh, my child, there you go again, asking me a question for which I can give you no answer."

Over the years, the old lady and her stories had not been able to satisfy the little girl's thirst for knowledge. And the question of the gods still troubled the child's heart.

One day—not long after one of the story-telling sessions with her grandchild—the grandmother died peacefully in her bed. At this, the little girl was very sad. Now she no longer had anyone to whom to direct her questions. After a large mourning ceremony in the house, her coffin was carried to the grave. But her stories remained in the girl's memory, as if death had no power to erase them. "O", thought the girl, "if only my grandmother hadn't died, I should still have been able to hear many stories about the gods from her, and have asked her much more. But now I have to find out for myself what the gods of the Sabeans and other gods are trying to achieve with their secretive ways."

The King of Sheba on his deathbed

The lengthy discussions about gods and their games of hide-and-seek with humans flared up anew as the girl's father lay on his deathbed. The entire family was gathered round, awaiting his testamentary instructions. The king's children were seated on armchairs lined up beside his bed. The king was sitting up in bed, propped up with cushions and holding his sceptre in his hand. The two small children sat motionless, as in the calm before the storm. Only the young girl with the dark chestnut-brown hair, who was somewhat older than the other two, seemed to know that at this moment something significant was taking place. Perhaps that was why she was so restless as she sat there. She was both sad and agitated at the same time. After a lengthy address to the family, the king shifted his gaze to the beautiful young girl sitting so restlessly on her armchair.

The King of Sheba on his deathbed. He is speaking with his daughter, the future Queen of Sheba, about the coming transfer of power.

"Do you wish to rule my kingdom, so that it will endure forever, my child?"

"Yes, father!" the girl replied.

"Will you see to it that my people will live in peace together with other nations, so that they will be spared from war, famine and sorrow?"

Without hesitation, the girl again agreed: "Yes, father!" "As representative of your people, will you be the first to make offerings to the gods of the Sabeans, so that the people of your kingdom will be united in their faith?" This time the girl reacted somewhat sharply: "No, father!"

"If you won't continue the Sabean tradition, I cannot install you as my successor."

Before the king had fully expressed his thoughts, the girl interrupted him: "What god has demanded a sacrifice from us? If you will show me his letter, saying that he demands it of us, then I will do it for your sake." His daughter's forthrightness did not really surprise the king. Since her childhood she had displayed the same keen spirit of enquiry. What should he say to her in his final hour, just as he was standing at the threshold of death, not knowing what awaited him thereafter? Should he to say to his daughter: "We have willingly sacrificed, because it appeased our consciences"? Or: "We have sacrificed, because our fathers before us did so, too"? His daughter might then well have replied: "If you sacrificed of your own free will, then surely I can of my own free will stop the sacrifices, don't you agree, father?"

What drove the king to demand of his daughter that she offer sacrifices to the gods after his death was fear, pure and simple. He wanted to ensure that even after his death the gods would remain well disposed towards him. He was afraid of dying and of what followed after. So he clung to the sacrificial rituals that had been handed down through the years as if this were the only life-raft available.

The King of Sheba wanted to ensure that his daughter, as the future queen, would operate in the same manner. So he had set those two conditions for her before she could become queen. Only if she gave her word that she would adhere to them all, was he willing to hand the sceptre over to her.

But his daughter evidently did not understand him. In his most difficult hour, she demanded evidence of him, and that even in writing. From where would he get such evidence? There were no written documents, because the gods of Sheba had written him no letter. Neither had an ambassador of the gods ever appeared before him. His father, grandfather, great-grandfather and great-great-grandfather had not received such a letter from the gods, either, because if they had, he would know about it. In the archives of his forefathers he had many letters from kings all over the world, but not one letter from the gods of Sheba or from those of foreign lands.

"My darling daughter, I have never received a letter from the gods. Nor has an ambassador from the gods come to me and said: 'You are to make offerings to the gods.' I have done it voluntarily, because they have been good to my parents, grandparents, great-grandparents and great-great-grandparents, since they appointed our family to nobility, as king and queen, prince and princess. Do you understand that?"

The girl replied: "Yes, father, I understand that very well! But it hurts me so when you offer the gods so much, yet the gods don't even find it necessary to come and collect your sacrificial gifts. They don't even say so much as a 'thank you' for your offerings. Is that not impolite? That's why I don't want to sacrifice to the gods of Sheba. I only want to sacrifice to those gods that return thanks and actually pick up the gifts offered to them."

The king was astonished at the wisdom his daughter displayed. He loved her sharp mind. He could rest assured that she would go down in history as a special queen on the world stage. In actual fact, he had no intention of bequeathing his kingdom to any of his other children. Traditionally, it was meant to go to his eldest child, but he wanted to make sure that his legacy would continue in his kingdom.

The girl persisted: "Father, do you even know the secret of the gods? If you do, I should really like to know." The ailing king stretched out his hand weakly toward his daughter and held her hands in his. Looking at her sadly, he said: "I have a long journey ahead of me. You, my child, will inherit my kingdom! Rule it with far-sightedness and understanding! As for the secret of the gods—I will only know that when I'm dead."

Before her father had quite brought out these words, the girl blurted out: "But father, how can I rule with understanding and far-sightedness if no-one can disclose the secrets of the gods to me? If you will only know their secrets after you are dead, then it will be too late for all of us. We need to know it now!"

"My daughter, from a little child you have shown courage and a sharp mind. How glad I am to have such a successor! I'm sure you will manage to get even the silent gods of Sheba to speak. If you do manage that, then please think of me, too, and ask them also to be kindly disposed to your father in the realm of the dead!"

When the king of Sheba died, his daughter was overcome by an immeasurable sadness. It was a sadness that could not be expressed in words, because her father had died without having revealed to her the secrets of the gods of Sheba. This realisation seemed to paralyse her. He was such a mighty king, but as his death approached, he was no different from the most miserable wretch. The tears ran unchecked down her red cheeks and moistened his coffin.

"Father, I will uncover the secrets of the gods! I will not die as wretchedly as you have—despairing, fearful and hopeless—because I am the Queen of Sheba! Oh, father, I understand that you want to please all the gods! I understand that you are in despair! But your daughter will not serve every god! Your daughter will find the mightiest god! You can depend on it, father!"

The girl is crowned queen

After her father's funeral, the girl was crowned as the Queen of Sheba in a grand ceremony. At eighteen, she was still in the flower of her youth when she ascended the throne.

Her acumen and understanding continued to develop further as the years went by. Her thirst for knowledge burned like a fire within her. Her grandmother, were she still among the living, would have said that her granddaughter had the most knowledge-hungry and enquiring mind of any child that the gods of the Sabeans had ever created.

Her subjects called her 'The Queen of Sheba'. She was breathtakingly beautiful and her land lay in the south, a place of bright, glaring sunshine. The extent of her realm was so vast that she never had the desire to conquer foreign lands. Her palace was like a castle in a fairy-tale. She only had to look out of the window to see the Indian Ocean lying at her feet. If she diverted her glance from the sea and looked through the windows to the north, she could see the small hills standing, not unlike her soldiers, in an orderly line before her. She wore the finest clothes, slept in the softest four-poster bed and never had to fear that she might experience hunger or thirst.

The Queen of Sheba was surrounded by experienced ministers and advisers. She liked to discuss the political management of her country with them, and was also open to new ideas and opinions. However, she tested their suggestions carefully and never blindly followed what they considered to be customary. In so doing, she caused her advisers many a sleepless night.

Conversation with the High Priest

One day the Queen of Sheba summoned the High Priest into her presence. For years he had been responsible for the sacrificial rites at the court. It had reached the queen's ears that he could even conjure up spirits and make contact with the dead.

As the High Priest stood before her, she asked him: "Tell me what you know about the gods of Sheba."

"Your Majesty, they visit me regularly when I summon them."

"How do you do that?" the queen asked in eager curiosity.

"My helpers and I gather at night and light a fire. Then we sprinkle the area with rosewater. Then our drummer begins drumming vehemently, while we dance and call on the gods to visit us. When the gods come, they transport us into another dimension, so that we lose our connection to this world. We no longer see what transpires in this world, but only the world of the gods. There are things there that we do not know in this world, such as unusual lights, in all manner of garish colours. Then they convey their divine powers to us, such that we can walk on hot coals without burning our feet. Through these gods we can even speak with the dead."

"That is truly interesting!" exclaimed the queen. "And then?"

"Then we converse with each other."

"How do you know that you are speaking with the dead?"

"They have exactly the same voices as the deceased."

"I find that hard to believe! So what do the dead say, then?"

"They say that we should obey the gods."

"What will happen if you don't obey?"

"Then they punish you. Once I was disobedient, and they gave me no rest during the night. They rattled the crockery in the kitchen. They even threw the cups through the air. Since that time, I have a terrible fear of the gods and their retribution."

"Are they really the gods that have made heaven and earth?" the queen enquired.

"They don't say that, but they claim to be the rulers of this world."

"Can they do anything other than being destructive?"

"That I don't know, because I don't wish to make contact with these gods again to question them."

"Do all the gods in Sheba instil such fear in people?"

"Yes, without exception."

"And what might their names be?"

"I don't know anything more about them."

The queen found it impossible to believe what the High Priest had told her concerning the gods of Sheba. If the gods only pursue evil, then where does the good come from, that after all also exists in this world? Because the High Priest was unable to answer this question, she did not take his words seriously. There had to be a trustworthy answer to explain both the good and the evil in this world, the beauty and the ugliness. Only then would what was claimed about the gods be trustworthy. But she knew of no-one who could answer these questions clearly for her.

A new report

One day, one of the customary receptions, held for ambassadors from friendly lands, took place in the great hall of the queen's palace. The queen was seated in the magnificent room, sceptre in hand, while to her right and left her advisers and ministers took their seats. The closer to the queen a minister or adviser was seated, the more important was his role, and the higher was the regard he enjoyed at court.

Among her servants, too, there was a ranking, which was clearly indicated by their uniforms. At such receptions the queen's cupbearer served only her and the important guest from abroad, as a sign of hospitality and high regard. The remaining servants of lower rank waited on those guests seated further away from the queen. They ate and drank from golden bowls and goblets, as they exchanged polite pleasantries. At the conclusion of the meal the conversation turned to political topics, the primary concern of which was the peace and friendship between the two nations. Still later, the immediate topical issues of the visit were discussed, and then towards the end of the reception, private or quite trivial matters were exchanged in conversation.

When the core issues for discussion with the queen had been debated and dealt with, the ambassador from Babylon, evidently pleased, expressed satisfaction at the outcome of his visit. His comment during their discussions——"Let us be wise, like the wise King Solomon" —had not escaped the queen's notice. She would have liked to know from where this wise King Solomon had acquired his wisdom. As was the custom after every reception, they would stroll in the palace gardens and engage in private conversation. That would provide the best opportunity to come back to the question of Solomon's wisdom. The queen was curious about it, just as in her youth, when her grandmother had told her all kinds of tales.

At the conclusion of the reception, one of the ministers took on the role of showing the members of the ambassador's entourage the sights of the palace. The queen herself strolled through the park in the company of the ambassador from Babylon, as he told her of his trips to Israel. Finally she asked him: "Is this King Solomon so wise that he can explain the enigmatic ways of the gods of Sheba?" The ambassador looked at the beautiful Queen of Sheba as if he were very happy to give an account of the wise sayings of Solomon, which had also made a deep impression on him. The gaze of the Queen of Sheba rested expectantly on the ambassador. "Ah", he said, "His wisdom is like a spring of clear water! He can explain everything, yes, even the furtive ways of the gods of the Sabeans."

The Queen of Sheba was deeply moved by these words. "What do you know about his wisdom?" she asked straight out.

"Your Majesty, it is a delight to be in the company of such a man and to converse with him. With his wisdom, he opens the door to a world to which few people ever have access," explained the ambassador.

"What kind of world?" she asked. "A world of evil gods?"

"No, a world of understanding. When you are in his presence, you get the impression before long that he must have been an observer for a time at the creation of the world."

"Then he must also be able to explain all the secrets of the gods," she concluded impatiently.

"He is even in contact with his living God." At this, the queen stared in amazement at the ambassador.

"But that's amazing!" she burst out. "Please go on! I can hardly believe it!"

"His God appeared to him in a dream and offered him a free wish: 'Ask what you want me to give you!' Solomon asked for an understanding heart, so he could know how to rule his people with justice and decide between what is good and what is evil. And behold, his god was pleased with his request, because he had not asked for riches or a long life or the death of his enemies. Not only did he receive an understanding heart like no other before him has ever had, nor anyone in future will ever have; but he also received on top of that everything he had not asked for, namely riches and honour like no other king on earth ever enjoyed in his lifetime."[2]

The Queen of Sheba was speechless with astonishment. If even the ambassador of mighty Babylon spoke like this, Solomon's wisdom must indeed be great. She was overcome by a desire to see this wise king with her own eyes and to hear his wise words. It was possible that he held the key to her questions, which no-one in her kingdom could answer. How often she had asked her grandmother why the god of the Sabeans did not reveal himself to his people. How often she had needed to be consoled by her with the thought that the answers to her questions were not knowable! The secrets of the gods could not be unveiled.

Since the reception for the Babylonian ambassador, the Queen of Sheba was curious about the wisdom of Solomon. More than anything, she wanted to know from his god why he condescended to comply with the wishes of the king. However, the queen was not a naïve woman, who believed everything she was told. Others could believe what they wished, but she preferred to rely on her own intelligent judgment. The story of Solomon that had been reported to her seemed somewhat incredible, after all. Was this all perhaps just a rumour,

---

[2] 1 Kings 3:5–14

a bubble destined soon to burst? Perhaps the Babylonian ambassador was merely exaggerating. She wondered if it would not be better to test everything for herself, before trusting another.

The queen's inner restlessness

Solomon's wisdom was the only thing occupying her innermost thoughts over the following weeks and months. Even if she found it hard to believe, she longed to hear everything personally from Solomon's mouth. She was especially interested in his god, with whom he was seemingly in contact. Perhaps his god could also answer whether hail could indeed be traced back to the wickedness of humanity. She thought long and hard how she could test Solomon—perhaps he, too, was only telling people stories and fables, as her grandmother had done. What the High Priest had dished up to her about the evil gods of Sheba was so unbelievable, that she had already almost forgotten this story.

Something was driving the queen on—the thought of this Solomon, who was unknown to her, had taken deep hold of her. So much so, that one fine day the queen ordered her subordinates to make preparations for a journey to Israel. She wanted to travel there, together with her royal court, and unveil the secret of the god of Solomon there and then. She took with her everything she would need on the journey. But beyond that, she had also thought up a long list of riddles which she wanted to present to Solomon, in order to examine His wisdom thoroughly.

An arduous journey is no longer an obstacle

She also remembered how in her youth she had been prepared to give the gods of the Sabeans everything, if only they would reveal themselves. Sheba was a rich land with much mineral wealth. The queen lacked nothing. The news that the god of the Jews was in contact with Solomon impressed her so much that she was willing to bring this wise king her most precious gifts. His god must be a mighty god, she thought to herself, after all that she had heard about him.

With her royal household, the Queen of Sheba travels thousands of kilometres across the desert, in order to reach the wise King Solomon.

After a lengthy journey through the desert with her caravan, the Queen of Sheba finally arrived in Israel. She rode upon her special camel, with golden decorations on the saddle which shimmered in the glaring sunshine. The camel's harness was also set with precious stones. The cloth draped across the camel's back, beneath the saddle and hanging down to the belly of the animal, was decorated with intricate needlework. Its edges were also adorned with golden tassels. She sat elevated on her camel as they approached the city gate of Jerusalem.

Her ambassadors had already arrived in Jerusalem three days earlier, to announce her coming at the court of Solomon. Now Solomon's servants were lined up in front of the city gate like pearls on a string, to welcome the queen. When the Queen of Sheba realised that the servants and chariots of the king were waiting for her before the city gate to escort her into the city, it took her breath away. Never, in any land she had visited, had a royal Majesty received her outside the city's gate with such a gesture of respect and courtesy.

Hastily she alighted from her camel. Before her foot touched the ground, a servant of the king offered her his hand to make the descent easier. Having greeted the queen with a friendly smile, the servant turned to her royal entourage with a sincere greeting of welcome. Then he escorted her to a golden chariot. Solomon's servants helped to transfer the queen's luggage from the camels to the chariots that stood lined up in a row.

What a sight! The travellers from afar first glimpse Jerusalem, the city set on a hill.

A long convoy of decorated horses, servants in uniform and golden chariots began to move in the direction of Solomon's palace. The king's camel drivers brought the queen's camels into the stables. As they noticed the approach of the royal chariots, the people on the streets of Jerusalem cleared a path for them and craned their necks at the side of the road in an effort to get even a short glimpse. The magnificent horses with their decorated manes pulled the golden chariots of the king with a loud trot. The people waved to the occupants of the chariots and shouted for joy, because once again something out of the ordinary was taking place on the streets of Jerusalem.

There was no end to the Queen of Sheba's amazement. She thought to herself: How much must his people love Solomon, if they even go out onto the streets and cheer, as soon as the royal chariot merely appears in the streets. She could not recall ever having received so much attention from her own subjects.

The royal chariots proceeded along the streets past the masses to the palace of Solomon. This stood out, by its size and splendour, from all the other buildings in Jerusalem. As the chariot came to a halt in front of the palace, the queen alighted. She looked about her as if she found herself in an exceedingly beautiful dream, from which she was reluctant to be roused. She saw a sublime palace, the likes of which she had not expected in her wildest dreams—made of precious timbers and gold.

Accompanied by Solomon's servants and her own court entourage, she made her way up the steps. From there she enjoyed a view of a world that almost caused her to lose composure. It was one in which she would have been happy to remain forever. She was initially led into the throne hall, which was lined with costly cedar wood from floor to ceiling. The queen was speechless as she noted the many pillars along its walls. Six steps led up to the throne of gold, which was adorned on either side with a lion. Beside the armrests of the golden throne stood two more golden lions.

The Queen of Sheba enters Jerusalem in Solomon's golden chariot. The citizens joyfully greet the visitors from afar.

The first encounter with the wise king

"King Solomon, I have heard that you are considered to be the wisest man ever born! That is why I have come here to you through the vast desert with my caravan. It is why I have tolerated the desert storms, and subjected myself to many dangers. I have foregone the comforts of my beautiful palace and instead camped in oases, and all this to hear the wisdom from your own mouth. My heart does not desire the treasures of this world and my soul seeks eternal peace, o wise king. What I have heard about you has moved me deeply, and it has now brought me here to you!"

"Oh beautiful Queen of Sheba, welcome to my palace, which is open to all who thirst for wisdom," Solomon answered in a friendly manner.

During this greeting the queen's servants carried 120 hundredweight of gold, and all manner of spices and gemstones, to the king as her guest gift. They spread it all out at his feet—right there before the throne.

When Solomon had thanked her for the costly gifts, a lively conversation struck up between him and the queen. Meanwhile, King Solomon ordered that a reception feast be prepared for the queen and her train. The conversation continued for hours, yet they did not run out of things to discuss. The more he related, the more she wanted to hear. He showed her his huge and magnificent palace, the best of the best. He also took her to the forecourt of the temple that he had caused to be built for his God, the God of Israel, and there he told her how his workmen had brought the hewn stones from the quarry and the best cedar wood from Lebanon. He also described in detail how they lined the floor and the walls with it, so that the stone was no longer visible. He continued by explaining how he had had the entire Temple of his Lord overlaid with gold. He pointed out the pillars, skilfully painted with cherubim, palms and flowers, as well as the exquisite carvings from costly timbers—everything that could be observed on the outside of the Temple. As she saw all this, she gained an inkling of what the interior of the Temple might be like.

King Solomon receives the Queen of Sheba before his throne. She presents him with 120 talents of gold as a guest gift.

The Queen of Sheba found her heart almost stopping in amazement. She had seen many kingdoms, but the wealth she saw in Jerusalem in Solomon's palace and at the Temple of his God far surpassed all her expectations.

However, the queen had not come to marvel at Solomon's wealth and wisdom, but rather to test him. She had come up with all manner of riddles that hardly anyone in her country was able to solve. At certain times she had asked her sages and ministers, but no-one had been able to give her the correct answers.

Might he be able to solve the riddles?

During the course of the evening meal, the queen asked King Solomon: "Can you answer one question for me?" "Ask me whatever you wish to know," the king willingly agreed.

The Queen of Sheba began:

"There is a king who deceives all suitors for the hand of his daughter. He says to them: 'I have two pebbles in a bag, one white and one black. If you can pick out the white pebble with your eyes closed, you may marry my daughter.' But only the daughter knows that he is deceiving the men by placing two black pebbles into the bag. One young man loves the king's daughter very much and asks for her hand in marriage. As every other time, the king places before him the bag containing the pebbles, but the daughter has already confided to him that the bag contains two black pebbles. How can he outwit the king, in order to marry his daughter?"

King Solomon grinned. "Ah, the man removes one pebble from the king's bag and throws it far away. Then he says to the king: 'There, now you only have the black pebble in the bag!'"

"One more question, Solomon. Two argumentative people are quarrelling, both claiming to know everything. Which of the two is wiser?"

Solomon and the Queen of Sheba dining together.

"Only the one who knows the origin of the lie, and of love, is the wiser."

After several more questions, which Solomon answered wisely for her, she said:

"Tell me the secret of how you came to have this wisdom that others don't have?"

"It is a gift from my God, because He is the source of all wisdom."

"Tell me, King Solomon, what is the most important thing in life to have: a kingdom, freedom or love?"

"O beautiful queen, what good is your beauty to you if you have no freedom; what good is freedom to you if you lack virtue; what good is your kingdom to you if you lack love; what good is love to you if you lack wisdom, and what good is all your wisdom if you have not recognized the source of wisdom, your God?" answered Solomon.

Amazed at Solomon's wise words, the Queen of Sheba thirsted to know more and more. Finally she said:

"So, please permit me to remain in your presence and hear all your wise sayings, until my soul is satisfied by your wisdom. I want to ask you everything I have on my mind, because only a truly wise person can provide me with satisfactory answers! I know of no-one in my country who could do this.

"See, your people on the streets are beside themselves for joy when they catch sight of you. What have you given them that they greet you with such gladness, and shout for joy?"

"I have given them neither gold nor silver, but I rule and judge them with the wisdom of my Lord, so that they enjoy peace."

"So you are also the judge of your people?"

"Yes, everyone who cries out for justice can come to me to participate in my dispensation of justice. And so every day people come to me with legal disputes and receive just judgments."

"Can I also observe how you judge the disputing parties?"

"Of course; it will not remain a mystery for you."

"Don't you have a judge in your country who can settle disputes?" the queen asked.

"Oh yes, a good many, even. But in a situation of testimony versus testimony, only wisdom can judge justly." "What does wisdom have to do with justice?" she continued to enquire.

"A great deal, o queen! We humans have a natural tendency to self-centredness. Just as we think that everything that is to our advantage is good and just, so we reject everything detrimental to our interests as evil

The reception in Solomon's palace for the Queen of Sheba's entourage.

and unjust. If our understanding of right and wrong is also determined by our self-serving nature, we will soon be in danger of establishing our own desire as the measure of justice. Many rulers of the nations have, for selfish reasons, done exactly this, making their own will the benchmark. But this is not justice in God's eyes. Justice should ensure harmony in interpersonal relationships. If that is present, it will lead directly to peace. Its absence signals unrest, rebellion and war. That is why it is so very important to me, that my people are judged justly."

The Queen of Sheba recognised more and more how well-grounded and reasonable Solomon's thinking was. Everything she learned from him amazed her beyond measure. Just as it is usual to greet one another on first meeting, the queen initially tested Solomon with a riddle when they first met in the palace. She asked her questions so skilfully that it seemed as though these had spontaneously flashed across her mind, because they always related directly to the conversation at hand. However, she had previously spent long hours at night, at home in her palace, thinking about her riddles.

Solomon found particular pleasure in her eagerness for knowledge. Whenever there was a lull in her riddles, he would ask if her spirit of enquiry had now been exhausted.

"No, Solomon, I have another question!" she answered one day. "A child said to an old man: 'Your thoughts

are my thoughts and my thoughts are your thoughts!'
What does that mean?"

Once more, Solomon smiled to himself as he heard
the queen of sheba testing his wisdom again and again
with new riddles.

"I will tell you, o queen, what you are getting at. It is the
bond of love that allows all the differences between two
human beings to dissolve into oneness."

The queen's mouth dropped open in astonishment. She
gazed at him for a time in amazement, before asking:

"Why has your God given you so much wisdom, and so
much less to other mortals? Is your God not unjust?"

"Ah, queen, now you're posing the same question that's
put to me by all those who do not know the true God.
To our limited understanding, it does seem unjust that
I should have received so much wisdom and wealth
from God, while so many others have only known pov-
erty and misery. But do you believe that my God will
allow His poor creatures to come away empty-handed?
Consider the animals; they know nothing of our troubles and concerns. Some of them live for just a short
time, without ever having known what was going on
in the wider world. They spend their life within a tiny
area, and then they die without ever grasping the bigger picture. Similarly with us; because we can't see or
comprehend that life will only be truly complete after
death, we shouldn't prematurely judge our fate. Being

only partway down the track, we are still unable to see the destination of our life's journey. So, without having the whole story, we should not hasten to dismiss God's plans as unjust."

Once again, the queen had to concede that Solomon was right. How true it was, that one should never rush to judgment before having heard the full story! She pondered the many times she herself, impatient, had made hasty, instant judgments.

The discussions deepen

During such conversations with the Queen of Sheba, Solomon decided to introduce the queen to the world of his God—much as one might dive down into the forbidding depths of a well to try to investigate more closely the reflection of the moon. He recognised a certain level of fear in the queen whenever the conversation turned to gods, but saw that she could temper this fear with her reason.

What would move a mighty queen to travel with a cumbersome caravan from Sheba to Jerusalem in order to test Solomon with riddles, if not her searching spirit, that sought to examine ancient traditions and values? Was it hatred of the gods, or love of them? Actually, she didn't seem to feel love towards the gods of Sheba, it was more like terror. Just as her high priest had been gripped by fear when the subject of the gods came up, so for her. The gods made her deeply uneasy.

Their unseen power had robbed many among her people of their reason. That was why she felt revulsion for the sorts of conceptions of the gods that people formed in their imaginations.

Now she was hearing something completely different from Solomon. In detail he told of how the God of his people, Yahweh, had created the world and the people in it. In the Garden of Eden, God had given them a wonderful environment. They had everything in abundance, and sorrow, sickness, want—yes, even death—were completely unknown. God had given them only one single prohibition; they were not to eat the fruit of a certain tree. Were they to do so, they would have to die. It's hard to fathom, but they allowed themselves

The Queen of Sheba questions Solomon in his palace garden.

to be tempted by the devil and, despite God's warning, they ate of the tree anyway. What God had said now came to pass. They became mortal and reaped for themselves all the evils that plague us all today. From that moment on, there was toil in work; there was sickness and despair; and enmity, hatred and death.

Many years later, after they had been expelled from the garden, their descendants gave rise to the many different tribes and nations of the earth. Then he told of Noah, and God's judgment on the people through a great flood. She heard for the first time about Abraham and the covenant that Yahweh made with him. The blessings of God for Jacob, of whose life under God's grace she had likewise never heard, filled her with profound astonishment at the fact that mortal humans could encounter God in this way.

At just such a riveting moment she suddenly interrupted the king and cried: "But what you're telling me is incredible, Solomon! You're not only capable of coming up with wise thoughts and words, you can also tell fables about the history of your people."

This time it was Solomon who was surprised—at the level of her doubt. He could, however, appreciate how astonishing and incomprehensible his information must be for her; up to this point in her life she had only ever known of the dead and imaginary gods and their statues, unable to accomplish anything.

Solomon continued his discourse: "I am living proof before your eyes that my God, o queen, has accomplished it all. As yet, you have not learned the whole truth about my God—what wonders He showed His prophets as signs of His almighty power! It will move you even more deeply."

These earnest and intense discussions left her no time to test Solomon with further riddles, as she had enjoyed doing in the early days after her arrival. He was giving her so much new information and material, and much of it needed to be clarified and expanded. So she would now spend endless hours in the palace garden with the king in deep conversations.

At night, when she retired to bed in Solomon's palace, she wondered whether she should also test this god Yahweh, whether He did in fact create heaven and earth. The clearest sign of His existence would surely be a miracle. She longed to see something like that with her own eyes.

Through these long conversations the queen learned that Solomon's God had caused Moses to write down God's laws, so that His people would learn what was right and wrong. In this way, they would know what God's commandment was for a particular circumstance. Anyone who broke God's laws had to sacrifice an animal according to the severity of his or her deed. People also brought thank offerings to the Temple. She realised that Solomon's people brought offerings from entirely different motivations than her own people did.

"Solomon, our High Priest told me that he can even make contact with the dead. I felt quite ill as he told me about such strange things. I would be interested to know what your God has to say about such activity."

"Among our people, also, there have from time to time been individuals not satisfied with what God has committed to us. They turned to evil powers and consulted them, and they even had dealings with the dead. So it became necessary for God to give a clear word, and therefore He commanded His people:

> "There shall not be found among you anyone who burns His son or His daughter as an offering, anyone who practices divination or tells fortunes or interprets omens, or a sorcerer or a charmer or a medium or a necromancer or one who inquires of the dead, for whoever does these things is an abomination to the LORD. ... You shall be blameless before the LORD your God".
>
> (Deuteronomy 18:10–13)

"How grateful I am for this clear pronouncement. I had myself felt that the practices of the High Priest instilled fear, and so could not spring from a good source."

The conversations in Jerusalem prompted a spiritual fermentation process in the heart of the Queen of Sheba. Just as the grape juice in the barrels bubbled and rumbled, so doubts, questions, incomprehension and curiosity rose to the surface, and at night robbed her of restful sleep. One day she could not hold back from again critically questioning Solomon.

"If it is as you've told me, why has the God of Israel not put an end to this fallen humanity? Wouldn't it have been good if He had created new human beings?"

Solomon smiled at this and continued: "I can't give you a clear-cut answer to that question, because God has not explained it. But please consider an important principle that applies to every action of God: **He never makes a mistake!** You only ever make new what has completely failed. Were God to have set aside the first human beings and created new ones, He would have signalled thereby that it hadn't been done well in the first place. But the day will certainly come when we will find out more about this."

Solomon continued after a short pause: "O queen, let me say this: God has found *another solution*. Step by step I will consider this with you. For this, both your patience and your acumen will be indispensable.

"You see, o queen, our God Yahweh has at any given time always revealed to humanity just as much as they could comprehend. And He will continue to reveal His plans for the world, step by step. The history of our people Israel began with Abraham. God had called Him and promised Him:

'And I will make of you a great nation, and I will bless you and make your name great, so that you will be a blessing … and in you all the families of the earth shall be blessed' (Genesis 12:2–3).

When Abraham's descendants were slaves in Egypt, they knew that a Saviour would free them from the yoke of slavery, but when and how that was to happen, was still unknown to them."

"Solomon, I can see that your faith in your God is downright unshakeable. But I find the fact that your God left other nations to their fate, and did not raise up prophets for them, simply unjust. Surely He could have shown His compassion to every nation, just as He did for the Israelites? After all, according to your claim, we are all His creatures. Then we would not be leading such miserable lives in darkness and ignorance."

"Queen, you forget one thing. The first humans lived far longer than we do today. Adam and Eve lived so long that they lived concurrently with children and grandchildren, up to and including the eighth generation. That means that Lamech, the father of Noah, still knew His ancestors Adam and Eve. That's how humans had the opportunity to learn about God's glory from Adam and Eve as eyewitnesses for 930 years. Only these first two humans saw with their own eyes how beautiful and perfect God is and how wonderful His original creation had been. They both had the opportunity to recount to their children and children's children in minutest detail what their previous life as sinless humans, in God's direct presence had been like—even though this wonderful period in the Garden of Eden was relatively short.

Despite this, Adam's son Cain, in the very next generation, became a renegade. While Noah and his contemporaries were born after Adam's death, he nevertheless would have heard reliable accounts about Adam and Eve from his father Lamech. Noah lived another 350 years after the great Flood, which is how he managed to see a considerable number of his descendants, nine generations in all. Abraham's father Terah still knew Noah, and Abraham himself was a contemporary of Noah for 58 years. And so they had every opportunity to get reliable accounts about the time before the Flood. But already back then the descendants of Noah had multiplied into many tribes and nations, so that they would have lost direct contact to Noah.

"Due to this isolation, the nations also lost the knowledge about God, replacing it with whatever took their fancy. On closer examination, it's clear that God gave mankind a reliable source of information as proof of his existence right up to Abraham's generation, namely in the person of Noah, rather like a living history book. If someone at that time were seeking God, he would be able to learn the truth from Noah, who was still alive at the time, along with all of his descendants. But people often forget the most important thing in life if they only busy themselves with seedtime and harvest, buying and selling. Then they blame God for leaving them in the darkness of ignorance, instead of asking themselves why they have not sought out the true God."

"But that's amazing!" exclaimed the Queen of Sheba. "How right you are!"

Solomon continued: "Wait, just be a little patient. You haven't even heard the most amazing part yet. Noah had three sons who survived the flood with him—Shem, Ham and Japheth. Even though important facts about God were available to the tribes and nations that descended from these sons of Noah, they turned to imaginary gods of wood and stone. Even Abraham and his father Terah were no exception to this.[3] God intervened to protect mankind from the darkness of ignorance. He spoke with Abraham and led him out of the land of Ur. God made an everlasting covenant with him, and so Abraham became the father of the faith. He is also the father of my people. Other nations also stemmed from Abraham. From the beginning, they all had the same opportunity to hear about the true God from a reliable source. First through Adam and Eve, then after the flood from Noah, and finally from Abraham. Your people, too, the Sabeans, did not preserve the truth about God and instead wandered down the wrong path of many gods of their own imagining. Those nations also that stemmed from Abraham's son Ishmael have turned to imaginary gods and gods of wood. Only the line of his son Isaac and his grandson Jacob preserved the truth about God."

"Is this God Yahweh angry with the other nations, because we have turned away from Him?"

"Of course it grieves God that the nations have turned from Him. But the worst thing is your worship of idols

---

[3] Joshua 24:2 –"Thus says the LORD, the God of Israel, 'Long ago, your fathers lived beyond the Euphrates, Terah, the father of Abraham and of Nahor; and they served other gods."

and the fact that some nations even sacrifice their children to idols; all that is an abomination to Him."

"Why does He not make a covenant with us, like He has with your people?"

"He already declared to us through Samuel: 'Those who honor me I will honor, and those who despise me shall be lightly esteemed' (1 Samuel 2:30). Truth comes from only one single source, but falsehood has a thousand sources. This single source of truth is God Himself.[4] And you can find it in Israel, because the Israelites are the witnesses to the living God, and they have His written word. Every other source produces lies that come from Satan and false prophets, from shamans and gurus.

"If God had made a covenant with every nation, then each nation would claim God for themselves, which in turn would lead to religious conflict. If the truth were then to get lost across the generations, they would still insist that their corrupted religions came from God. And so they would have misused His covenant for their false teachings and lies. Don't the nations to this day still fight over the claim that their fabricated religion comes from the true God?

"In spite of this, He has not rejected these nations, but invites them to recognize the truth. Our God Yahweh has always warned us that He did not choose us as

---

[4] Psalm 36:5 –"Your steadfast love, o LORD, extends to the heavens, your faithfulness to the clouds."

His people because we were more numerous than all the other nations (Deuteronomy 7:7), but because He blessed Abraham out of love and promised Him that He would make a great nation out of His seed.[5] He chooses what to us seems insignificant, in order to glorify Himself through it and thereby to reveal Himself. We are Abraham's descendants. Our God has seen and heard the suffering and misery of our people in Egypt and has therefore taken pity on us. The time is still coming when He will bless every nation in His own way and His own time."

"But why have you not made this truth known to the other nations through your ambassadors? How many years have you lived here in Israel, keeping yourselves apart from other nations and tribes, and you even go into battle against them in the name of your God? What does your God say to that? I don't get it! You see, if the first king of your people, or your father David, had at least written a letter to my father, the king of Sheba, then he would have known before he died who was the true god, and he would not have had to live with the fear of death."

"O, queen, how impatient you are! Did His chosen people ever understand His plans and commandments in such a way that they could have gone to the other nations as trustworthy ambassadors of the true God? What harm Israel has caused by its disobedience to God, since it first left Egypt! It's not enough to know

[5]   God said to Abraham (Genesis 15:5): "Look toward heaven, and number the stars, if you are able to number them.' Then he said to him, 'So shall your offspring be."

the true God, because Satan knows Him too; our life and behaviour need to be godly, also. That's the very area in which we, His stubborn people, have repeatedly and tragically failed. This is why God commanded us not to marry the daughters and sons of the pagans. We have this weakness, that we tend to readily abandon our true God and follow after the strange gods of other nations. We have not learned our lesson yet."

"Well and good! You say that your God made heaven and earth. What about our sun- and moon-god? Didn't they create anything?"

"No, as a matter of fact they created nothing at all. They exist in the imagination of many nations as 'true gods', but they only fill the people with fear."

"If it's as you say, how can one tell the true God from the false gods?" asked the queen.

"That's a very good question. Every person should seek the answer to it before it's too late, instead of only focussing on earthly things; because even a beautiful life without knowledge of the true God leads to a state of eternal lostness.[6]

"The first radical difference between the true God Yahweh and the other gods is the fact that we cannot fathom Yahweh from the perspective of our fallen humanity. Every image of God that we make for ourselves

---

[6]　How one can escape from this lost condition is described in detail in the Epilogue part III.

leads us into error, because while human beings are inclined to think of God as big and mysterious, they don't necessarily see Him as inclined toward us. Such a view of God makes Him unpredictable and therefore fear-inspiring. But the true God is our helper in good and bad times. He is good and just.[7] He reaches into our lives, and He concerns Himself with our troubles and sickness, if we ask Him to. That's because He is a living God."

The queen interrupted him: "In Sheba, people believe that the gods have pre-determined our lives and so we must live them out that way and only that way, until eventually we die."

Solomon continued: "If that were so, we would be nothing more than puppets. Despite our evil deeds we would then be innocent. But Yahweh made men and women with a free will. He does not even intervene when we pursue evil. He permits it, but He warns us not to call evil good and good evil. We cannot understand all His ways, which is why He says to us through the prophet Isaiah: 'For my thoughts are not your thoughts, neither are your ways my ways, declares the LORD. For as the heavens are higher than the earth, so are my ways higher than your ways and my thoughts than your thoughts' (Isaiah 55:8–9). What I find so marvellous is that He is the source of all truth: 'You are God, and your words are true' (2 Samuel 7:28)."

---

[7]   Psalm 25:8 — "Good and upright is the LORD; therefore he instructs sinners in the way."

The Queen of Sheba reflected on Solomon's description of Yahweh's nature. Then she asked the king: "Does that mean that Yahweh does not ask us to make human sacrifices?"

"That's right! Neither your children, nor you, need to die for God, in order to find mercy and approval in His eyes. He also does not want you to feign faithfulness and obedience toward Him, while at the same time you pursue evil towards other people."

Agitated, the queen countered: "But I have heard that there are gods who demand of people that they offer their children and themselves in sacrifice to them, so that after death the souls of people will not suffer torment."

Solomon and the Queen of Sheba in animated discussion on the Mount of Olives.

"O queen, 'All the gods of the nations are idols!' (Psalm 96:5). Our God Yahweh is like a good father and shepherd to all mankind. We need not kneel before Him in fear as before a despotic king. Only slaves have to do that before their masters. We are made in His image, creatures bestowed with love and dignity. We do not have a spirit of slavery, which is why we do not have to submit unconditionally to His will, like slaves."

"Solomon, with those words you've addressed exactly what's been going on in my heart and soul over all these years. Up till now, the depictions of the gods in my country have kept me from serving them. In my innermost being I felt nothing for them. But what you say about your God Yahweh gives expression to all my emotional stirrings."

Her conversations with Solomon caused the Queen of Sheba repeated moments of deep reflection. At first, her questions had been critical. But as her stay in Jerusalem went on, she had come to see how well off Solomon and his people were. His God was no silent god who sat in a temple, incapable of movement, like the gods in her country. His God had shown Himself to be a friend who had given the king his immensely valuable wisdom upon request. And on top of that He had also given him wealth in abundance. This God, she realised, also thinks of orphans, widows, the poor and aliens, so that they are not oppressed. Even the animals that work for people are not forgotten; they are not to be denied their fair share of food by way of being muzzled, for example.[8]

This God seemed to her like a friend, a counsellor, a judge and protector to the people of Israel, all wrapped up in one single person. As she studied the commandments of Moses, she understood how good Yahweh's commandments were, in that they rejected evil and commanded good.

As the queen came to realize these things, her discussions with Solomon took a distinct turn. Up until now she had taken a critical approach, but this now swung towards respect. Now she was no longer the accuser of the God of Solomon, but rather one who, stumbling around in the darkness, found herself reaching for the king's helping hand.

She was glad that with his wisdom Solomon had removed from her eyes the veil of which she had been unaware all these years. She had had a self-righteous way of looking at things, but because of her power and authority, no-one could reproach her for it. It was Solomon's humility toward the lowly which actually revealed his superiority. He demonstrated his wisdom not through theory, but with his love, and the actions that flowed from it.

The visit of the Queen of Sheba brought about the meeting of two towering personalities: a queen and a

---

[8]   Deuteronomy 25:4 – "You shall not muzzle an ox when it is treading out the grain."

king, both of whom had enjoyed a conservative up-bringing, in order to preserve the traditional value system at their respective courts. But God had made a new man of Solomon, one who did not conform to the expectations of the queen's world. Many a one in Solomon's position would have been offended and hurt in his pride if someone had tested his wisdom with riddles. He, however, did not find it offensive; rather, he answered every question of the queen frankly. He realized full well that she was also testing his God, from whom he had received his wisdom, with her riddles. The queen was amazed that Solomon's God seemed to have such a clear understanding of things, much more so than her own.

Her newfound insight did not escape Solomon. He took delight in conveying Yahweh's wisdom to her step by step, and in the amazement it caused her. What she understood of Solomon's God and His commandments was in perfect accord with her heart and soul. She also concluded that the things which she did not understand about his God must also be good.

The Queen of Sheba's stay in Jerusalem was like balm to her soul. Solomon didn't only show her the sights of his city, he also accompanied her in his golden chariot, to show her something of the blossoming land of Israel. On occasion, they sat down for a while in a suitable spot, to make the most of the panoramic views of Jerusalem. They sat quietly viewing the city silhouetted against the skyline, as one admires a beautiful painting.

Spring had also made its contribution by enveloping the fields surrounding the city in bright colours—as if it, too, wanted to fill the queen's heart with joy. All these excursions, as far as to the Sea of Galilee, were experiences of a special kind for her. She could even discern Solomon's wisdom in the stillness of nature, where she could continue their interesting conversations.

As they were listening to the splashing of the waves at the Sea of Galilee, many questions came into the queen's mind, which she simply could not hide from Solomon. Her eyes were firmly fixed on the king's lips, in order not to miss any of his wisdom.

"Solomon, you spoke yesterday of *another solution,* when I expressed the thought that God could have created a new humanity. What is that solution?"

"God already told the first two humans of His plan. Addressing the deceiver, He said: 'I will put enmity between you and the woman, and between your offspring and her offspring; he shall bruise your head, and you shall bruise his heel' (Genesis 3:15). How this solution would unfold in detail, this first human couple had no idea as yet. For them, this message was still too encoded, but in it they could discern that their deceiver would one day be defeated."

The queen said: "I have seen such extraordinary things here in your presence, and what you have said must be of God. So you must be a special king in God's eyes, in His plan. I should very much like to know more about that."

The line of descent of the Messiah

"I'll gladly explain to you how God introduced us step by step into His plan. With the very first announcement of salvation to Adam and Eve, God had explicitly promised that the Messiah, who would be victorious over the devil, would come from the seed of the woman—and not the man. That indicates a very special line of descent, because there is no mention at all of a male parent. After several generations God found an obedient man in Noah. On God's instructions, he built a huge barge to save both his family and all the land creatures and the creatures of the air, whilst the rest of humanity, who had become evil, perished in the Flood. Noah had three sons: Shem, Ham and Japheth. God's free choice fell upon Shem, and with that his descendants, the Semites, were destined to be the bearers of the continuing line of blessing. At the same time, two thirds (Hamites, Japhethites) were excluded from this line, but not from the possibility of salvation. To the Semite Abraham, God had said that He would make Abraham's offspring great and so make a people for Himself.[9] With that, Abraham became the first citizen of the nation of God, which today we call Israel. God said to him: 'In your (= Abraham's) offspring shall all the nations of the earth be blessed, because you have obeyed my voice' (Genesis 22:18). This choosing of Abraham once again narrowed the range of people groups from which the Messiah was to arise, by hundreds. From Abraham's several male de-

---

[9]   1 Chronicles 17:22 –"And you made your people Israel to be your people forever, and you, o Lord, became their God."

scendants (Genesis 21:3 and 25:1–2), God's choice fell upon Isaac. Then of Isaac's two sons, Esau and Jacob, the latter was chosen: 'A star shall come out of Jacob, and a sceptre shall rise out of Israel' (Numbers 24:17b). God has announced the continuation of this line of salvation through His prophets , updating it again and again. A plan of salvation that has been precisely fulfilled, and will also continue to be precisely fulfilled, is unique to the true God of the Bible. Then the coming of the Saviour from the family of Jesse was prophetically foretold: 'There shall come forth a shoot from the stump of Jesse, and a branch from his roots shall bear fruit' (Isaiah 11:1ff). Jesse had eight sons; God's choice fell on David, the youngest of them, from whose descendants the Messiah was to come: 'I will raise up your offspring after you, who shall come from your body, and I will establish his kingdom. He shall build a house for my name, and i will establish the throne of his kingdom forever' (2 Samuel 7:12–13). My father David had an impressive nineteen sons, and God has confirmed me as a member in this line of salvation: 'Of all my sons (for the LORD has given me many sons) He has chosen Solomon my son to sit on the throne of the kingdom of the LORD over Israel ... . I will establish His kingdom forever (1 Chronicles 28:5,7).'"

"I am astounded, Solomon. So you have also been brought into this line of salvation planned by your God. What a privilege! How wonderful everything is that I'm learning from you, and also who you are."

"In Micah 5:2 the prophetic words of God finally focus on a single location:

> 'But you, O **Bethlehem** Ephrathah, who are too little to be among the clans of Judah, from you shall come forth for me one (= Messiah) who is to be ruler in Israel, whose origin is from of old, from ancient days.'

So God clearly showed us ahead of time that we don't need to seek salvation anywhere else."

"Solomon, please tell me: why does a Saviour or a Messiah even have to come? What's the reason? What is the Messiah even meant to save us from?"

"It's our wrong conduct toward God, our evil deeds, our wrongdoings, as well as everything contrary to God's requirements and which rejects God. God groups all of that together under the one word: *Sin*. Sin is really bad in the eyes of God because it offends His holy justice, and the justly deserved consequences for us are punishment and separation from Him. We humans know of no way to remove sin. But if sin is not first removed, we can never attain to God or enter His kingdom. For the removal of sin, God has once for all determined: someone who is absolutely sinless must take all the sin of mankind upon himself and pay the price of our punishment with his own death. Then and only then can our sin be forgiven on the basis of this act."

"But is there even such a person, who is sinless and who could do this for us?"

"No, there is no such person. And God has told us this, over and over:

- 'For there is no-one who does not sin' (1 Kings 8:46).
- 'Who can bring a clean thing out of an unclean? There is not one' (Job 14:4).
- 'They have all turned aside; together they have become corrupt; there is none who does good, not even one' (Psalm 14:3).

But there is *one single person* in God's Heaven, able to fulfil the three indispensable requirements for this rescue mission. He is sinless, and He is also prepared to follow through with this saving act. And thirdly, it must take place here on earth, because here on the earth is where humanity fell into sin. It is this One who is God's *Messiah*!"[10]

"Solomon, that all sounds truly fascinating. But tell me, how will people know that He is the Messiah and not merely some charlatan?"

---

[10] Messiah: The Hebrew word 'mashiach' used in the Old Testament means 'the anointed One' (Messiah). In Israel, priests and kings were installed in their office with a festive anointing with oil. (Exodus 29:7; 1 Samuel 10:1) The term 'anointed one' was originally only used of the king. In the prophetic Word, the prophets later saw a coming king from the line of David, an 'anointed one', who would be both priest and king in one person. He is the worldwide Saviour of humankind out of its lost condition. Even in one of the oldest books of the Bible, the book of Job, we read: 'I know that my Redeemer lives' (Job 19:25). And this Redeemer is the Messiah.

"Queen, He is distinguished by a **three-fold seal**. This seal is absolutely forgery-proof, so that at His appearance He will be unmistakeable. His identity will be unequivocal, so that even the most skilled falsifier would not be able to impersonate Him. When I now name these three seals for you, you will see that no-one can imitate them:

"**1.** *His character will be perfect:* 'He is altogether lovely' (Song of Solomon 5:16). No-one before or after Him will ever display a flawless, balanced character like His. Its excellence will not be impaired by pride or rashness, and His wisdom will not be marred by even the occasional folly. His objectivity will not be distorted by any prejudice, and His justice not adulterated through selfish whims. His dignity will be in accord with His humble bearing. He will lovingly care for others out of compassion, not through being driven by anxious concern. His zeal will not spill over into frenzy, and His patience, though immense, will not overlook anything of importance. His tactful dealings will not cause others embarrassment, without thereby being in any way insincere. His dealings with others will be completely open, yet always appropriate. His authority will be in harmonious accord with His goodness, patience and mercy.

"He will never have to retract His words with the comment, 'I didn't mean it like that'. He will never have to change His teaching due to newer findings of which He was previously unaware—because His teaching is from God. He will never have to confess a sin, because

He will be the one and only sinless person ever to have walked on the earth. He will never have to admit to having made a mistake, because He will always act in line with God's will. He will never lose His patience and say something rash. Many people will come to Him with their questions—men, women and children, religious and irreligious, prostitutes and deceivers, politicians and merchants, poor and rich, respected and despised—to all He will always give the right answer, the one that conforms to the will and the Word of God. He will be the perfect teacher, who Himself lives out what He teaches. Nevertheless He will **also** be one of us in the truest sense of the word—'Son of God and Son of Man.'"

"Solomon, I can well understand that there has never been such a man. Certainly no-one could imitate that. This seal alone is enough to single Him out from a multitude."

"But God has added two further seals, so that everyone without exception can know that He alone is the true Messiah", continued the king:

"**2.** *He will do signs and wonders:* The Messiah will be inimitable in His working of miracles. Wherever He goes, many medically incurable people will come to Him and He will spontaneously heal them: 'Then the eyes of the blind shall be opened, and the ears of the deaf unstopped; then shall the lame man leap like a deer, and the tongue of the mute sing for joy' (Isaiah 35:5–6). The world has never seen anything like it. This sign will be unique in all the world.

"**3.** *He will sacrifice Himself to save mankind:* The removal of sin involves unimaginable suffering of body and soul. In the end, the Messiah will have to suffer a disgraceful death. But by that very death He is enabled to offer salvation to many billions of people. They simply have to accept God's verdict of being lost in sin and ask Him to forgive all their sin. In this way the Messiah will become their personal Lord and Saviour and He will confess their names before God, because He has atoned for their sins.

"Isaiah prophetically foresaw this agonizing death that was needed to enable salvation:

> 'Surely he has borne our griefs and carried our sorrows; yet we esteemed him stricken, smitten by God, and afflicted. But he was wounded for our transgressions; he was crushed for our iniquities; upon him was the chastisement that brought us peace, and with his stripes we are healed. All we like sheep have gone astray; we have turned everyone to his own way; and the LORD has laid on him the iniquity of us all. He was oppressed, and he was afflicted, yet he opened not his mouth; like a lamb that is led to the slaughter, and like a sheep that before its shearers is silent, so he opened not his mouth. … . And they made his grave with the wicked … although he had done no violence, and there was no deceit in his mouth (Isaiah 53:4–7,9).'

"In short", the king continued, "We can cling to the fact that: 'The Spirit of the Lord shall rest upon him, the Spirit of wisdom and understanding, the Spirit of counsel and might, the Spirit of knowledge and the fear of the Lord' (Isaiah 11:2).

"Solomon, did I understand you correctly, that this so-very-exceptional person has to die?"

The death of the Messiah

"Yes, He will even die a particularly horrible death. The prophecy indicates that His hands and feet will be pierced in a brutal manner. 'For dogs encompass me; a company of evildoers encircles me; they have pierced my hands and feet' (Psalm 22:16). To adequately describe the infuriated crowd and its leaders requires the imagery of wild and aggressive animals: 'Many bulls encompass me (= Messiah); strong bulls of Bashan surround me; they open wide their mouths at me, like a ravening and roaring lion' (Psalm 22:12–13). You see, queen, how dreadfully He will be treated. Before they put Him to death, they will even scramble for His clothes—God has foretold us even such details: 'They divide my garments among them, and for my clothing they cast lots (Psalm 22:18).'"

For what seemed a long time, the queen was unable to utter a word. What she had just heard moved her deeply and at the same time it seemed incomprehensible. Finally she opened her mouth: "But Solomon, that's terrible! Tell me, will no-one want to prevent this? Surely He must have many friends among the people, if He has given many incurably ill people their life back?"

"Queen, no prophet has foretold that anyone will save Him from His distress. I can't understand it either. Regrettably, it will be as Psalm 22:6–7 prophetically declares: 'But I (= Messiah) … am scorned by mankind and despised by the people. All who see me mock me; they make mouths at me; they wag their heads.' But queen, consider this: if the Messiah were not to die in our stead, no-one could be saved. As hard as it is for us to accept the thought that God requires death for the atonement of sins,[11] it is nonetheless a fundamental reality, that we can only be given eternal life through the death of the Messiah."

"Truly", said the queen, "I can barely grasp that thought. As I see it, it should be enough for people to do some kind of good deed–to agree on a compensation deal with God, so to speak. Won't that do, so long as one is truly sincere?"

"It's good that you're at least thinking about how we might stand righteous before God. Many people will in fact go down the path of attempting self-redemption. That's the approach of the many religions of the nations. There you can see everything that human imagination has been able to come up with. But nothing devised by human beings will help anyone. We stand on and remain in the Word that God gave directly to the

---

[11] Genesis 2:17

prophets for us, and which they promptly wrote down for us. In this way, we've received direct and irreplaceable information from God that is even available to us as a written document. This, by the way, also shows you that there is only *one* true and living God. All the gods of the heathen nations are idols—they can neither speak, nor do they have a message for us humans which could help us order our lives aright."

"Now you're addressing what I already said to my grandmother and to my father: 'Did the god of the Sabeans ever personally express himself—either orally or in writing?' Both of them had to deny this. Now I hear for the first time of a God who has revealed Himself to people. He has made direct contact with people, and what He has said is available to us in the form of written documents. Never before have I heard such a thing."

"Queen, now you have realised something of fundamental importance. Do not trust any god that has not addressed human beings directly and spoken to them. Gods that do not do this are mute: 'Their idols are like scarecrows in a cucumber field, and they cannot speak; they have to be carried, for they cannot walk. Do not be afraid of them, for they cannot do evil, neither is it in them to do good' (Jeremiah 10:5). One thing is certain: 'All the gods of the peoples are worthless idols' (Psalm 96:5).

"But I must tell you one more important fact about the Messiah: although He knew no sin whatsoever, He will be made sin in our place. None of us is so right-eous that we could stand before God, but through His suffering the Messiah earned for us the righteousness which God accepts. You can imagine that this will be an unimaginably difficult task for the Messiah, fully to take upon Himself our mountain of sin, to suffer death as our penalty and so to remove our sin totally and completely.

"Through Isaiah, God tells us that the Messiah will forgive even the worst kind of sin if only we turn to Him in faith:

> 'Though your sins are like scarlet, they shall be as white as snow; though they are red like crimson, they shall become like wool' (Isaiah 1:18).

> 'I have blotted out your transgressions like a cloud and your sins like mist; return to me, for I have redeemed you' (Isaiah 44:22).

"God made all this known to the prophet Isaiah, who describes it for us in such words as if it had already been accomplished:

> 'You have burdened me with your sins; you have wearied me with your iniquities. I, I am he who blots out your transgressions for my own sake, and I will not remember your sins (Isaiah 43:24b-25).'

"What Isaiah says there is remarkable. God's plan, to carry out the work of salvation through the Messiah, is certain. It is so unalterably fixed that even the timing is expressed as having already taken place. But Isaiah's words tell us even more. 'I blot out your transgressions! You have burdened **me**!' In the person of the Messiah, God **Himself** accomplishes all justice and righteousness, and in so doing removes all sin! The Messiah is a human being, but He is nevertheless of divine nature and lineage, which means He is different from all other humans since Adam. And with that, another word of Isaiah's takes on special significance. He announces the birth of the Messiah in this way:

> 'Behold, the *virgin* shall conceive and bear a son, and shall call his name Immanuel' (Isaiah 7:14).

"She calls her son Immanuel, and that means 'God with us'. The announcement by Isaiah actually includes the fact that the Messiah, who is of divine nature, is born of a virgin. The woman who gives birth to the Messiah is enabled in a wonderful way by *God Himself* to do so, and not by any earthly man."

"What are you saying there, Solomon?" said the queen. "Did I hear you correctly? A *virgin* is to have a child? But that's unheard of! Could it be that you're now telling me the latest of your country's legends?"

"Unheard of ... yes! In that, you are absolutely correct, queen. But consider; God is ever able to do things of which we have otherwise not heard. Have you ever heard that the sun stood still in the sky for several hours[12] and did not move on by so much as a finger's breadth? God did this in answer to a prayer of Joshua, and in all these years He has never done it again. I can also tell you here and now that after Messiah is born, it will never happen again that a virgin will have a child."

"Solomon, it must be something really stupendous, for this Messiah who will appear among you in Israel to step in for the offences of the people. I confess that a trace of envy is stirring in my heart. How fortunate your people are, that this Messiah is coming to their nation. Is all this grace meant for you alone? Will all the other nations remain empty-handed, even though we are many more in number?"

The Messiah is the Saviour not just for Israel, but for Gentiles, too

"Would you have become Queen of Sheba if my God, the maker of heaven and earth, had not chosen you and raised you up? I'm sure that at the appointed time He will send us to the other nations as His ambassadors, so that the Gentile nations will come to honour His name. He has not reviled other nations. There have repeatedly been people who have regarded the Israelites as their people, who have acknowledged Yahweh as their God. There was a Moabitess called Ruth, who lived amongst us. But God will in the end also have compassion on the other nations. He won't leave them in ignorance; rather, in the end, there will be people out of all the

---

[12] Joshua 10:12–14

nations of the world who will worship Him as the one true God."[13]

"Yes, I'm very interested in that. Please tell me more!" said the Queen of Sheba.

"Our God remembers all the nations of the earth. His care and consideration is so all-encompassing that no tribe or language or nation will be excluded from His salvation. So that you don't think I'm just trying to put your mind at ease, I will use the very words of God as spoken through the prophet:

'I (= God) will make you (= Messiah) as a light for the nations, that my salvation may reach to the end of the earth' (Isaiah 49:6b).

"Can you now see that God does not exclude any people group from His salvation? And specifically, to the nations apart from Israel, God said earlier through the prophet:

'I am the LORD; I (= God) have called you (= Messiah) in righteousness … for a light for the nations' (Isaiah 42:6).

"God has explained His world-encompassing plan of salvation, which will be offered to all nations, like this:

---

[13] Psalm 22:27 – "All the ends of the earth shall remember and turn to the Lord, and all the families of the nations shall worship before you." Psalm 86:9 – "All the nations you have made shall come and worship before you, O Lord, and shall glorify your name."

'So shall He startle many nations … for that which has not been told them they see, and that which they have not heard they understand' (Isaiah 52:15)."

"Oh, Solomon, that truly is good news. I am extremely happy that no-one is excluded, and that includes us Sabeans. You have already told me so much about this Messiah, I can barely grasp it. But I'm still thinking about one thing you mentioned the other day: He is to be born of a virgin! How can a virgin bear a child, and a person, at that, who is so totally different from us? She is, after all, a completely normal woman, who can therefore also only bring a completely normal person into the world."

"Queen, I shall try to explain it to you. Just as you can only pick apples from an apple tree and figs from a fig tree, so a normal woman can only bear a normal human child to a normal man–you are quite right in that. But this child will not be conceived through a human father, but by divine activity. The prophet describes the mystery of the incarnation of the Messiah, and of His nature, with the following words:

'For to us a child is born, to us a son is given; and the government shall be upon his shoulder, and his name shall be called Wonderful Counselor, Mighty God, Everlasting Father, Prince of Peace. Of the increase of his government and of peace there will be no end, on the throne of David and over his kingdom, to establish it and to uphold it with justice and with righteousness from this time forth and forevermore' (Isaiah 9:6–7).

"We're dealing here with a real human being, but that does not tell the full story. This extended description of this child goes well beyond all that is human–because this child comes from eternity. He is the Messiah! The prophet denotes Him as a king with an imperishable and therefore eternal kingdom."

The Messiah is ruler over an eternal kingdom

"God has given the kingdom to the Messiah: 'I have set my King on Zion, my holy hill' (Psalm 2:6). And the prophet Daniel says: 'To him was given dominion and glory and a kingdom, that all peoples, nations and languages should serve him; his dominion is an ever-lasting dominion, which shall not pass away, and his kingdom one that shall not be destroyed' (Daniel 7:14). That is why the prophet Zechariah could announce the coming of the Messiah as that of king as well: 'Behold, your king is coming to you' (Zechariah 9:9)."

The Messiah is also God

"Queen, what I am going to tell you now will complete-ly take your breath away. In Psalm 2:7 God says to the Messiah: 'You are my son'. That equates Him with God. The Messiah that will be born of a virgin will therefore be both at the same time: He is coming to us as both man and God. You can also put it this way: He who is God will become a man–and He who is man is also God. Are you still with me, Queen of Sheba?"

"Solomon, give me a moment to think. What you say is unprecedented. I'm fast approaching the limits of my own reason."

"Queen, I understand only too well. I also needed much time to come to grips with those revealed thoughts of God which are well beyond our human reckoning. Just to explain it to you another way, let me mention a statement from a psalm written by my father David:

> 'The LORD says to my Lord: 'Sit at my right hand, until I make your enemies a footstool for your feet' (Psalm 110:1).

"At the start of our discussions I presented to you several of the links in the chain making up the line of salvation. Accordingly, the Messiah is called David's son as far as His human descent is concerned. But in this psalm, David calls the Messiah His **Lord.** How can He be both David's Lord and at the same time also be called David's son?"

"Solomon, your wisdom well-nigh makes me giddy– the ways of your God transcend all my thinking. This is one riddle I can't solve; you will most definitely have to help me out here."

"See here: the Messiah, from His human descent, *was* David's son. But because the Messiah is God, as I have already explained to you, He is therefore also David's Lord. In other places the Messiah has three different divine names ascribed to Him, which are all names of the living God:

- Jeremiah 23:6 – 'This is the name by which he will be called: The Lord (= Yahweh) our Righteousness.'

- Psalm 45:6 – 'Your throne, O God (= Elohim), will last for ever and ever.'

- Psalm 110:1 – 'The Lord says to my Lord (= Adonai): …'

This highlights once more the fact that the Messiah is one and the same as God. And so the prophet Zechariah could rightly say: 'Then the Lord my God (= Messiah) will come' (Zechariah 14:5b)."

"Solomon, I have learned a lot from you now. What gives me most joy is the fact that the Messiah of your people will also be the Saviour of my people. Then your God will also be our God. O, this trip has most certainly been worthwhile!

"But there is one thing I still don't understand: you said the Messiah had to die for the people's sin, but then you also said that He was an everlasting king. How will He then escape from this death-trap, to enable Him to be this king?"

"O queen, once again you have followed with perceptive thinking. This question obviously had to come. But God has answered it for us through my father David in Psalm 16:

> 'You (= God) will not abandon me (= Messiah) to the grave, nor will you let your Holy One (= Messiah) see decay' (Psalm 16:10).

"So God will bring the Messiah back from the grave–He will arise from the dead! The Messiah is the Eternal One! Just like God, He too was from eternity and will continue through all eternity. The prophet Micah testifies to His eternal existence:

> 'But you, Bethlehem Ephrathah, though you are small among the clans of Judah, out of you will come for me one (= Messiah) who will be ruler over Israel, whose origins are from of old, from ancient times' (Micah 5:2)."

"Solomon, now another question occurs to me: Is this God not able to bring us back to life too, even when we have been dead for a long time? That would certainly be a hopeful perspective, given the finality of death."

"Queen, your thinking is certainly astute–the Messiah will one day abolish death entirely. God has already told us that through Isaiah: 'He will swallow up death forever' (Isaiah 25:8). In Psalm 68 God revealed to my father that 'Our God is a God who saves; from the sovereign Lord comes escape from death' (Psalm 68:20)."

"Will all people be allowed to find this salvation through Messiah?"

"O, yes, queen, God has promised that also. Through the prophet Joel He says:

> 'And … everyone who calls on the name of the LORD shall be saved' (Joel 2:32a).

"So what is His name, then?"

"God has not yet revealed His actual name; that will only happen shortly before His birth. But many of His titles, which describe Him very accurately, have already been mentioned by the prophets. Let me just remind you of Isaiah 9:6 alone: Wonderful Counsellor, Mighty God, Everlasting Father, Prince of Peace."

"Solomon, why does He not tell us His name, so that we are already able to recognize Him at once by that?"
"O queen, just imagine for a moment: if God had already disclosed the name of the Messiah a thousand years in advance, then many families would have given this name to their newborn sons. Some ambitious people among them would even claim to be the Messiah in order to capitalize on it. But you may be certain it will be a very special name."

"Solomon, I have to admit that your God must be very far-sighted."

The all-knowing God

"Queen, our God Yahweh is not only far-sighted, but wise and all-knowing as well. He knows all things ahead of time, right down to the smallest detail. He even knows at this moment just how our life will progress. He has even recorded in His Book of Life[14] the names of all those who will one day love and honour Him. God has revealed to my father David something that will amaze you. He put this on record for all people and for all time in Psalm 139:16:

'Your eyes saw my unformed body. All the days ordained for me were written in your book before one of them came to be.'

You can imagine that these thoughts were overwhelming for my father, too, and that he could only acknowledge humbly in response:

'How precious to me are your thoughts, O God! How vast is the sum of them!' (Ps. 139:17)."

"If He already knows my life in advance, is there then no possibility for me to shape and change my life for myself?"

---

14   Daniel 12:1b –"But at that time your people—everyone whose name is found written in the book—will be delivered."

"But yes, certainly, queen! You need to consider two things:

1) You can ask God to guide your steps and direct your ways, to influence those things you cannot. There are many things in our life that we can't prevent, and others we would dearly wish to see happen. To us, our lives seem to pass unalterably. But that's where our God is prepared to guide us in the correct path. God revealed that to me directly and I have recorded it in Proverbs 16:9:

> 'The heart of man plans His way, but the LORD establishes His steps.'

"Isn't it wonderful, how God is prepared to intervene in our lives and smooth paths which we in our own strength could otherwise never have traversed! He is able to guide our steps in specific ways, and open doors that to us seem to be totally shut. Because God is a merciful and loving God who only means us well, we can do no better than to commit ourselves to His gracious leading.

2) On the other hand, God has placed us into a freedom that knows no equal. The tyrants of the earth use their might to subjugate people. This restricts people in their actions and enslaves them. Even though our God is almighty, He nevertheless permits us to act freely. He has created us as free agents, who can shape our own lives. And just think: Everything that we do and decide in all freedom is also known to Him in advance.

Even these very days are in one sense already recorded in His book, as if it had all already taken place. Putting it another way; that part of our life's story which still lies ahead of us, as yet concealed in darkness, is even now fully known to God."

"Solomon, once again I need to take a deep breath. I feel as your father David once felt: These thoughts are too difficult for me; with the best of intentions I cannot grasp them!"

During the course of these days the queen learned more new things than ever. Even though she was especially gifted at following complex reasoning, these discussions demanded her utmost concentration. Nonetheless, all the conversations with Solomon during their excursions into the regions surrounding Jerusalem invigorated her soul and refreshed her intellect, like summer rain on parched earth. At the end of the day, it delighted the Queen of Sheba to have finally received definitive answers to all her questions.

One day brought an additional pleasant surprise. Solomon was invited to a wedding and he asked the queen to accompany him, in order to show her how weddings were celebrated in Israel.

They were received in a large, very festively decorated hall. People ate and drank, and sang and danced with abandon. The Queen of Sheba experienced a particularly lovely wedding in which the couple, dressed in white, were seated under a canopy. They, too, were clearly full of joy. When Solomon asked whether she liked what she was seeing, she replied full of gratitude: "I have experienced a very appealing marriage ceremony, in which your God played a central role. In my country the gods of the Sabaeans do not even get a mention at weddings. I have seen much that is new, and it was by far the happiest wedding I have ever witnessed."

The very next day, as they were seated on a bench in Solomon's palace garden, still speaking about the Jewish tradition, new questions arose in her mind.

Where do we come from?

"Solomon, something I must definitely still ask you: How long have there actually been people on the earth? While my grandmother was very knowledgeable, she had no answer for this question. But then perhaps your God knows this?"

"O queen, you surmise perfectly correctly. It is our God who has made everything, the stars and the vast expanse of the heavens, as well as the earth with everything that lives on it, which also includes us humans. Mankind began with the creation of one human couple; God has even given us their names. I have already mentioned that they were called Adam and Eve. Before God created people, He had the plan for it: 'Let us make man' (Genesis 1:26)."

"Hold it a minute there, Solomon, what do you mean 'let us'? What does that mean? Do you in fact also have many gods, as the Sabaeans believe?"

"Now you are asking about something very difficult to understand. We have only one God, but this one God has a son—as I have already mentioned. Whilst this son is a person in His own right, He is nevertheless one with God, so much so that it is entirely correct to speak of only **one** God. And this is how it is in our Scriptures, too—sometimes in one way, and sometimes another. The very first verse of the first book of Moses states that 'In the beginning God made the heavens and the earth' (Genesis 1:1). That sounds more like just one God, but even the Hebrew word God uses here to denote Himself—Elohim—is already in the plural form.

"Since you are now seeking to understand something this deep, I want to entrust something completely new to you. God has not told anyone this before. I am the first to be told, and it could make me somewhat proud, that God has disclosed to me a mystery that was well hidden until now, but I want to remain humble, because it is an undeserved gift from God. In my proverbs I have recorded this significant fact of creation: 'Then I was beside Him, like a master workman' (Proverbs 8:30a).Can you think who this Executor, this Agent and Master Craftsman mediating the entire creation process might be?"

"No, certainly not, all this is so new to me. Please don't torment me with curiosity. Tell me plainly and directly!"

"It is the Messiah!"

"O, that is truly hard to comprehend. Your Messiah seems ever bigger and bigger to me. First you tell me He will be the Saviour of your people Israel. Then you draw the bow much further and tell me that He will also be the Saviour of all the nations. And as if that were not enough you tell me He will heal every illness and even raise the dead. And now you add to it all by coming out with the revelation that He is the Creator of us all.

"Solomon, now I feel truly close to fainting! Who can grasp all this? I'm out of breath and I even believe that my heart stopped beating for a moment in astonishment. All these things I have discovered here with you! You are truly called of God. How good that I undertook this strenuous trip. I could not have sent a representative; I had to hear all this straight from your mouth. I could not have guessed even the half of what you have confided to me."

"Do you know, queen, that every detail of your person is a thought of the Messiah? You have such wonderful long and dark chestnut-brown hair, your attentive and beautiful brown eyes are lovely to behold. Your appearance is a delight for the eyes! Nothing about you is accidental, not even the curvature of your fingertips or the tip of your nose: 'He (= Messiah) has made everything beautiful in its time' (Ecclesiastes 3:11a) is how I wrote it in my book Ecclesiastes at God's direction. It is actually easy for me to apply this revelatory word from God very personally to you. Yes, I actually get the impression that God may be giving me an object lesson on beauty through you."

"Solomon, I have now heard so much sublime truth about the Messiah. Now I really don't know how I'm supposed to regard Him. Do I need to stand in fear of Him? How will He act toward us humans? Will He be stern or friendly; will He be waited upon, or will He perhaps even serve?"

"Yes, this question is certainly justified. As you already know, many of our fellow rulers are served by a huge royal court, and they expect their subjects to kneel before them and to fall down in the dust. Have you ever known any such subject to love such a king? Such kings only produce lackeys and flatterers. The Messiah is quite a different king: He comes to serve people, to help them, to heal, to love them and to save them from their sin."

"But there has never yet been such a king as this Messiah!"

"O, how right you are! Just listen to all that has been foretold about Him: The people of all the nations are plagued by fear of their gods and demons. The Messiah on the other hand says: 'Fear not, for I (= Messiah) have redeemed you; I have called you by name, you are mine!' (Isaiah 43:1b). People who belong to God sometimes feel that their faith has grown weak. Here, too, the Messiah steps in to strengthen faith: 'A bruised reed he will not break and a faintly burning wick he will not quench' (Isaiah 42:3).

"Many people suffer at the thought that they are unloved. The Messiah, however, shows us a love such as no person can possibly show to another: '…because you are precious in my (= Messiah's) eyes, and honoured, and I love you' (Isaiah 43:4).

"If we find ourselves in any kind of difficulty or need, He comes to our aid: 'When you pass through the waters, I will be with you; and through the rivers, they shall not overwhelm you; when you walk through fire you shall not be burned, and the flame shall not consume you.' (Isaiah 43:2).

"We humans often wander about helplessly and go astray, when we follow all manner of ideas. Here, too, the Messiah will lead us, just like a good shepherd leads His sheep: 'He (= Messiah) will tend His flock like a shepherd; He will gather the lambs in His arms; He will carry them in His bosom, and gently lead those that are with young' (Isaiah 40:11). And now let me tell you something else that shows the eternal love of the Messiah toward us. For all eternity we are engraved on the palms of His hands, those very hands that will have been pierced for us: 'Behold, I (= Messiah) have engraved you on the palms of my hands' (Isaiah 49:16)."

"O, but that speaks of an unimaginable love. In my country we do not know of a single instance, in which someone has loved people in such great measure. I am deeply impressed!"

The good shepherd

"Queen, I have already told you a great deal about our God. But there is still something very important to add. I must definitely draw your attention to the 23rd Psalm. God inspired my father to record this text, so that all following generations would also still be able to find comfort in these words. Listen carefully to them, if you will:

'The LORD is my shepherd;
I shall not want.
He makes me lie down in green pastures.
He leads me beside still waters.
He restores my soul.
He leads me in paths of righteousness
for his name's sake.
Even though I walk through the valley of the shadow of death,
I will fear no evil,
for you are with me;
your rod and your staff, they comfort me.
You prepare a table before me
in the presence of my enemies;
you anoint my head with oil;
my cup overflows.

Surely goodness and mercy shall follow me
all the days of my life,
and I shall dwell
in the house of the LORD forever.'

"This text speaks of a good shepherd. Can you think who this shepherd might be?"

"Solomon, you have explained so much concerning life and death, the King of Heaven, the Saviour of mankind, and always it was the Messiah. I guess that this time, too, it will surely be none other than this great Messiah?"

"How astute your conclusion is, once again. It is indeed the Messiah! By now you recognize the voice of this good shepherd in all my accounts. It is He who firmly leads us and protects us from all harm. When we are in His hand, nothing can ever separate us from Him: no war, no danger, no enemy, not even death itself can bring about a separation from Him."

"What are you saying there? Surely death is an absolute separation! Don't you know that?"

"Just take another look at this line: 'Even though I walk through the valley of the shadow of death, I will fear no evil, for you are with me.' (Psalm 23:4). Queen, I definitely need to explain this more closely, because it concerns our dying. As we die, we experience the loneliest moment of our entire existence. Whilst we are still on our deathbed, family members and dear friends may still be present. But in that moment when we close our eyes for the last time on this earth, not one of those who surrounded us in life will still be with us. Alone and forsaken, we then walk through that valley of death.

"But then comes the great surprise: A single person now steps up visibly and lovingly takes us by the hand. His rod and His staff will ward off all the powers of death, and we can know ourselves absolutely secure in His loving hand. You see, death does not have the last word. The Messiah is Lord over life and death, and that fact is now seen in all its reality. Death has been vanquished by the Messiah; only its shadow remains. But where there is shadow, there must also be light. And so it is here. No one is afraid of a shadow. The shadow of a lion cannot devour us, the shadow of a sword cannot kill us, and the shadow of death can do us no harm. That's why I fear no disaster, because the Messiah has a firm hold of me. With a firm step He brings us into the light—into the eternal sun. The prophet aptly describes this: 'The (present) sun shall be no more your light by day, nor for brightness shall the moon give you light; but the LORD will be your everlasting light, and your God will be your glory' (Isaiah 60:19). That is eternal life—to be always and forever with the Messiah!"

Deeply moved by these words, the queen could only say: "What a wonderful Messiah! He has even overcome death. I so very much wish that He will also be with me in my death. Then I will not fall into some indefinable darkness, but will experience His eternal light!"

Cut back to the previous days

One day the Queen of Sheba summed up her impressions so far, as she sat at the evening meal with Solomon:

"How fortunate you are, Solomon, you and your people! By now I have seen quite clearly that your God stands by you and your people, He blesses both you and the work of your hands, the fruit of your fields and of your animals. He blesses you richly with material goods; on top of that you have His promise, to support your people forever and to keep your enemies from overwhelming you. He promises your people to protect them, if they walk in His ways. It must be wonderful to have a God who relates to you as a trustworthy friend and partner! Who else can claim that? Truly, what I have learned about your God has left me speechless. I cannot comprehend it. I'll only digest it all once I am back in my country again."

"Do you wish to return home, queen?"

"Yes, Solomon! Over all these days that I have been your guest you have shown me how you honour your God. And you have honoured me, too, fed me and opened all your doors to me. I have been able to enter into your life as guest and observer, and plumb the depths of your wisdom. You have received me with humility and shared your wisdom with me. Everything impresses me, starting with your servants, who have served me in a humble and friendly manner, as though I were their queen, right up to your God, who has given me to understand, through His laws, that He has even remembered the foreigners in your land, how they are to be treated.[15] I thank you for your hospitality.

What has happened to me?

"And now, Solomon, I must confess something very important to you. Perhaps it won't even surprise you, because I have come to a far-reaching decision. It is something that has taken place in my innermost heart, and I want to share it with you first of all. I am now firmly decided to follow your God, just as you do. By now you know me well enough to know that I don't say something lightly. By patiently addressing all my seemingly endless questions you have brought me to this firm conviction: Your God is the only true God. He is so full of love and there is nothing about Him that arouses distrust, as with the gods of the Sabaeans. Your God has inclined Himself towards human beings, and He has truly spoken to them and in His commandments given them a good framework for living.

---

[15] Exodus 23:9 –"You shall not oppress a sojourner. You know the heart of a sojourner, for you were sojourners in the land of Egypt."
Deuteronomy 10:17–19 –"For the LORD your God … executes justice for the fatherless and the widow, and loves the sojourner, giving him food and clothing. Love the sojourner, therefore, for you were sojourners in the land of Egypt."

Only your God has given us written documents. And your God's Messiah is downright breathtaking. That He should willingly submit to death in order to save us for all eternity is hard for a human heart to fathom. Even if my capacity to understand is inadequate to grasp everything, I nevertheless believe all that your prophets have said about Him. My heart belongs to your God, who is now my God also. And your Messiah is now my Messiah as well."

At this, Solomon took the queen's hand and assured her: "You have truly become very wealthy. No-one in this world can become wealthier than to have found the true God. Everything in this world is transient—our wealth, our power, our reputation, our looks—only that which God has already given to us through faith will last into eternity. One day when faith becomes sight, we will realise the full measure of His mercy.

Solomon's treasure house

"Come, queen, after tonight's meal I still want to show you my treasury. Everything I will show you now is only a pale shadow of the riches that He has in store for us in His Heaven."

Together they entered a special room in Solomon's palace that had the appearance of a museum. As a servant of Solomon's opened the door, the queen's heart almost stopped. She was extremely impressed to see so many treasures all at once. Golden chests were filled with sparkling gemstones in every conceivable colour. Rings, diadems and brooches filled the treasure trunks. Golden goblets and bowls sat in rows on shelves. On the walls hung swords, bows and arrows made of gold, which Solomon had received as gifts from foreign kings. Silver did not even feature in his treasury, because it was not as highly valued. There were costly fabrics made of silk into which threads of gold had been woven. These melted the queen's heart. Then she saw the gold chamber; a room well-nigh overflowing with gold.

"Do you like it, queen?" Solomon asked.

"Yes, everything you own is beautiful and precious."

Solomon answered: "I want you to take pleasure in my wealth, too. Choose what your heart desires and I will give it to you."

"I like the golden goblets of your father David. The diadem, too, with the many diamonds, appeals to me."

At this, Solomon's servants brought together all the goblets and pieces of jewellery which the queen liked and Solomon handed them over to her with a generous heart. Then Solomon called his servant to him to also pack for the queen several chests with gemstones and costly fabrics, several golden candlesticks and much more. He even gave her his golden chariot that was decorated with gemstones. She received far more gifts from Solomon than she herself had brought for the king.

At this the queen was completely surprised. Her mouth could only utter a weak "But Solomon … ."

Solomon came toward her with his finger against his lips, to indicate she need say no more. Then he added: "You undertook that long journey from Sheba to Jerusalem, to seek out my wisdom with your own eyes, because you could not believe what you were being told. You wanted to make sure that you were not getting the wool pulled over your eyes, so you tested me with riddles. And then you brought me gifts richer than I had received from any other king on earth. With that, you honoured the wisdom that comes from my God. Do you think for one moment that my wise God would let you return to your country empty-handed? You acted correctly from start to finish. You did not allow yourself to be duped by earthly wisdoms. Nor did you let deserts and other obstacles deter you. You have seen how much my God loves His creatures, who have an alert spirit and use their minds in the manner that you do. It pleases my God immeasurably when we don't let His gifts get rusty, but polish them so that they sparkle like a diamond and, like a tree, bear much fruit. You looked for God and you found Him, by seeking and finding His wisdom in me. Just as I have today presented you with my riches, so He will give to you richly—both here and in eternity. He will bless you and protect you, and stand by you against your foes."

What is the greatest thing of all?

"Solomon, before I return to my kingdom, I would like to put several more questions to you: 'What do you think is the greatest thing in this world? Is it wealth, is it power, is it reputation, or is it wisdom?'"

"Queen, nothing of the kind can satisfy a human heart! The greatest thing is the certainty of being loved by someone wholeheartedly and then to return that love with the same intensity!"

"You have expressed that well, but how often in life does one come across such a love, that is returned in like manner and intensity?"

"Good point", replied the king. "It's far more common that someone falls in love with another person, but the other person is not even aware of it. Such one-sided love can wear down the heart and only gives rise to unnecessary longing. We call that lover's grief, and it's like a bad hangover.

"Reciprocal love that tends to keep on increasing in both parties is the most beautiful of all conceivable forms of love. When you seek this love it is like a person trying to fish in the Dead Sea."

"Solomon, do you mean to say that such love is impossible?"

"I can only give you one answer to that: 'With God nothing is impossible!' Queen, I must tell you something else. I have described for you the most beautiful of all forms of love, but in this fallen world everything has a side-effect. It is similar to medications. You take them to get well. But they can also trigger something negative in another area. But no-one would deny themselves healing because of the side-effects. You see, that is exactly how it is with perfect love. With every separation it automatically triggers a longing, and that in both parties and in equal measure. That is a law of nature in this world that can be expressed like this: *Longing for the other is directly proportional to love!* Conversely, therefore, you can measure the degree of love by the degree of longing. So always test a relationship by the degree of mutual longing!"

"Solomon, you once said that hope will come to an end because everything will have been fulfilled. Faith will come to an end because it will have become sight. The elapsing of time will cease, because it will pass over into eternity. So what will happen to love in eternity?"
"I can see that that question had to come. But I have an answer for you: Love will never cease, but in eternity it will be free of all yearning, because then there will be no more separation."

"Solomon, this love you describe—does it have anything to do with God?"

"O, yes! God is not only the inventor of love; He is even the original cause of all love, yes, more than that: He *is* love! I explained to you that true love is always mutual. That also applies to our relationship with God. He first loved us—even when we were still far from Him. He now seeks our love, so that this principle of mutual love is fulfilled. If we respond to God's love and love Him whole-heartedly in return, we experience the greatest of all possible riches. Then we will live with Him eternally."

"Solomon, can I learn another secret from you? Because of my position and power as Queen of Sheba, everyone acts as if they love me sincerely and appreciate me. But I am surrounded by a whole lot of yes-men. That's why it is difficult for me to distinguish true love from the feigned kind. I know that some people only love my fame and honour. So how can I recognize true love?"

"When someone sacrifices His life to save you, you can tell by that that it is not only true love, but also the greatest possible love."

"But Solomon, what use is it to me if I recognize this true love only *after* his death? I want to know it beforehand, before it is too late!"

"Love is the only force in this world capable of shifting priorities from the self to the other person. This process should be irreversible. But where a reversal does occur, we speak of the cooling down of love. Then all priorities revert to their original setting. By this you can discern true love from feigned love."

"I understand, but is it not true that even the greatest love in this world wilts like a flower out of water? Is it possible to stop this process?"

"As long as you don't mix good with evil it will flower forever. Because it's lying and deceiving, isn't it, that cause love to grow cold?"

"Solomon, even if you don't mingle lying and cheating with love, it will grow cold someday."

"Then it is a mute love, whose vocabulary and dimension don't extend beyond the oft-used and stereotypical phrase, 'I love you!' Such love all too often fizzles out after flaring briefly like a straw fire, with its ashes quickly blown away by the wind."

"Once again you've hit the nail on the head, Solomon!"

"God has given us the gift of speech. That clearly distinguishes us from the animal kingdom, because there you can find nothing of the kind. What do you think, if love is the greatest thing, then could there be a connection between love and speech?"

"O, Solomon, in the meantime I have been able to learn much wisdom from you. So now I can easily answer your question. Love must ever be newly articulated. However much you love and appreciate the other person, new words are always called for—accompanied by deeds. Love without words is like a house without a roof, like a meal without seasoning, like a day without sunshine. Who would want something like that?"

This description of love really appealed to Solomon. And he added two further significant points that characterize love:

- "The greatest love knows no boundaries, nor does it have conditions attached. A love based on demands and conditions is like a ship without a rudder. It would be better not even to set out on such a path."

- "Love can even be perceived with all five senses. When such love is mutual, it will last forever. Such love is perceived as most beautiful when each party loves the other equally and when both are always assured of this."

"Have you already found such a grand love, Solomon?"

"No, not yet."

"But why not, Solomon? You are, after all, the wisest man on earth!"

"While ever two people—or one of the parties concerned—cling to their self-centred interests and desires, such a magnificent love will forever remain a mystery for them. But I want to tell you about another great love, namely the love of my God for the people of the world. His overflowing love offers us eternal grace: 'I have loved you with an everlasting love; I have drawn you with unfailing kindness' (Jeremiah 31:3, NIV). Remain with Him and in His love. Does He reproach us for our sins? He could condemn us, but He doesn't do that. Because of His great compassion He will send the Messiah into our lost world, in order to offer salvation to all who want it with an honest heart. He can forgive a thousand times. He is not a God who quickly becomes angry and slams the door shut in our face. Many believe that He is totally out of reach, and that He savours His glory without ever caring about people; and that He only has eyes for the pious. So they construct a picture of Him as if He were a God full of prejudices, just as we are. The more wretched someone feels before Him, the more God loves that person. To reciprocate such love is the grandest thing in all the world. Whoever does that, will with Him be given all things."

The Queen of Sheba interrupted Solomon, before He could finish speaking: "But Solomon, how can I love God when I have never seen Him?"

At that he grinned and continued speaking, all the while smiling to himself:

"O, such a poor, miserable people! They rave about a rich uncle in Babylon, whom they only know from hearsay, and hope that one day He might remember his impoverished relatives and leave his fortune to them! If this were to come about, they would find it easy to applaud and embrace this rich but dead uncle in sheer gratitude and love. How much more would people pay homage to God, if they knew that He knows all His creatures and is prepared to give them His immeasurable wealth, if only one says, 'Yes, I will'. These poor creatures would rather cling to a straw and flirt with such thoughts. But about God they say: 'How can I love Him, if I have never ever seen Him?' Don't you see that this God has revealed Himself to people a thousand times over and given them endless prophecies? 'God is not man, that he should lie, or a son of man, that he should change his mind. Has he said, and will he not do it? Or has he spoken, and will he not fulfil it?' (Numbers 23:19). That is why one does not need to insist on seeing Him, rather one can trust His words and prophecies as a child trusts its father, even when He does not first prove to the child that He is right and that He means well. Is it not enough for you, queen, that you have heard from me of His goodness and His deeds?"

The Queen of Sheba surveyed Solomon with eyes wide with astonishment, which she then put into words: "How wise you are, Solomon! When I was told about the greatness of your wisdom, truly, I wasn't told the half of it."

Solomon thanked the Queen of Sheba sincerely for this high appraisal of his wisdom. He had grown fond of her curiosity and her alert mind. They had spent countless hours in animated conversation and discussion. Now it was her last evening in Israel, and the time had come to say farewell. The following morning, she would set out with her caravan and her court and return to her kingdom.

Departure

Next morning Solomon accompanied the queen as far as the city wall of Jerusalem. His servants loaded onto the queen's camels the gifts he was giving her. The sun was already spreading its comfortable warmth over all. A light spring breeze caressed the queen's long chestnut-brown hair as she turned to take her leave of Solomon. To him, however, it seemed as if she wished to stay a moment longer to ask him another one of her searching questions. When this expected question was not forthcoming, he knew for certain that all her questions had now been answered. Regarding the queen with a friendly gaze, he left her with these final thoughts for the trip:

"Before you leave Jerusalem, I still want to tell you something important about my God. Everything He says is true, and His commandments are just and completely in agreement with our conscience. His many prophecies, recorded in the books of His prophets, have in part been fulfilled very promptly—by that you can readily tell that the prophet has spoken God's words—and the remainder will be fulfilled at the right time with the same precision and certainty. By this you can see the difference between the words of the true God and the words of men with their invented gods. The idols are deaf and mute. But the living God has authenticated His prophets with miracles—or even gave them authority to do miracles, as for example

Moses[16]and Elijah[17]—so false prophets can be exposed very quickly. Queen, you are a clever woman. So you will not waste your time by worshipping false gods and idols."

"How shall I discern His righteous words from the words of mere humans?" the queen promptly retorted. "Quite simple! Place every word on the scales of your conscience. Then even a child will be able to see what is in accordance with the mind of God. His commandments prevent suffering and misery in this world, if we abide by them. You see, people cannot refrain from ly-

---

[16] God authenticated Moses by many miracles:
- Moses' staff becomes a snake and then a staff again (Exodus 4:2–4)
- The ten plagues in Egypt (Exodus 7:14–12:6)
- Israel led through the wilderness by a pillar of cloud and of fire (Exodus 13:20-22)
- The Sea of Reeds is parted (Exodus 14:1–22)
- The bitter water Marah becomes sweet (Exodus 15:22–25)
- The nation of Israel is provided with quail and manna in the wilderness (Exodus 16:1–36)
- A rock provides water after being struck by Moses with His staff (Exodus 17:1–7)
- Victory over the Amalekites (Exodus 17:8-16)
- Healing of Miriam's leprosy (Numbers 12:1–16)
- The earth swallowed Korah and those rebelling with Him (Numbers 16:1–35)
- A look at the bronze serpent saves from death by poisonous snakebites (Numbers 21:4–9)

[17] God also authenticated Elijah through many miracles. Some are named here:
- Elijah prophesies a lengthy drought (1 Kings 17:1)
- Miraculous supply of flour and oil for the widow at Zarephah (1 Kings 17:7–16)
- Elijah raises the widow's son from the dead (1 Kings 17:17–24)
- On Mt. Carmel Elijah calls out to God for help, and He sends down fire from heaven (1 Kings 18:30-39)
- Elijah predicts the death of King Ahaziah (2 Kings 1:1–17)
- Elijah divides the River Jordan (2 Kings 2:1–8)

ing and cheating. At the same time they are angry and shocked if they themselves are lied to and defrauded. Their conscience rebels against it, just as our God is opposed to it."

"How right you are, Solomon! That is true. We lie, but don't want to be lied to. We kill, but we don't want to be killed. Can we recognize God's commandments in that?"

"Yes, queen, that's exactly right! While the nations of the heathen have no prophets and no written records of God's messages, they nevertheless have God's commandments which He has placed into the conscience of every living person. Whoever listens to the voice of his conscience and acts accordingly, acts in line with the mind of the true God. But God knows that we rarely act in conformity with the voice of our conscience, but that we do to others the very thing that we don't want to have done to us. That's why He announced that the Messiah, who is yet to come, will save men and women from all the nations and tribes of the world."

The Queen of Sheba's difficult farewell at the city gate of Jerusalem

Difficult farewell

As the Queen of Sheba bade Solomon farewell, it was with a heavy heart, because she had grown accustomed to hearing His wise words and come to appreciate His wisdom. Before she said 'good-bye' to the king, she said to him, with a forlorn look: "Wise King Solomon, your words are nourishment for my soul! Therefore I want to do three things when I return to my kingdom:

I want to erect a magnificent memorial to the name of your God, so that my people will know that your God Yahweh is the true God for all people.

In your name, dear Solomon, I want to plant a tree, to bear sweet fruit, as sweet as the words that come out of your mouth.

I want to pass on your wisdom to my people, so that every child will know that we are not alone in this wide world—exposed to all the adversities of life—but that we have a God whose power extends to all peoples everywhere and whose goodness reaches to the widest heavens."

The caravan of the Queen of Sheba slowly made its way toward the south. For a little while longer, Solomon remained by the city gate as if rooted to the ground. He gazed after her, as her silhouette grew smaller and smaller, the further she moved away from

The Queen of Sheba's caravan on the return trip

him. "Ah, queen," he said to himself, "you came to test my wisdom, and you were massively amazed. And now you're going back to Sheba with a joyful heart, because you have found the true God Yahweh and have accepted the Lord of all peoples as your personal Lord also. But you have forgotten to ask me the most important question of all; namely how our God Yahweh will one day receive you into heaven. Perhaps you will return one day and put this question to me as well. If not, then I want to speak it into your heart: The most beautiful and greatest surprise of your life awaits you there!"

Jasmin Yildiz

The biblical text relating to the Queen of Sheba's journey

The following Bible text from **2 Chronicles 9:1–9, & 12** formed the basis of the creatively fleshed-out story 'The Queen of Sheba's journey—from a historical perspective', as well as the sermon 'The Queen of Sheba's journey—from a New Testament perspective'.

> *Now when the Queen of Sheba heard of the fame of Solomon, she came to Jerusalem to test him with hard questions, having a very great retinue and camels bearing spices and very much gold and precious stones. And when she came to Solomon, she told him all that was on her mind.*
>
> *And Solomon answered all her questions. There was nothing hidden from Solomon that he could not explain to her.*
>
> *And when the Queen of Sheba had seen the wisdom of Solomon, the house that he had built, the food of his table, the seating of his officials, and the attendance of his servants, and their clothing, his cupbearers, and their clothing, and his burnt offerings that he offered at the house of the LORD, there was no more breath in her.*
>
> *And she said to the king, "The report was true that I heard in my own land of your words and of your wisdom, but I did not believe the reports until I came and my own eyes had seen it. And behold, half the greatness of your wisdom was not told me; you surpass the report that I heard.*

Happy are your wives! Happy are these your servants, who continually stand before you and hear your wisdom!

Blessed be the LORD your God, who has delighted in you and set you on his throne as king for the LORD your God! Because your God loved Israel and would establish them forever, he has made you king over them, that you may execute justice and righteousness.

Then she gave the king 120 talents of gold, and a very great quantity of spices, and precious stones. There were no spices such as those that the Queen of Sheba gave to King Solomon.

And King Solomon gave to the Queen of Sheba all that she desired, whatever she asked besides what she had brought to the king. So she turned and went back to her own land with her servants.

The only life-story in world history that was ever foretold

Over the centuries, many people have crossed the global stage who have influenced the world with their good or bad deeds, and have secured for themselves a spot in the history books. They became known as emperors, like *Julius Caesar*, or *Charlemagne;* as commanders of conquering armies, like *Alexander the Great,* or *Napoleon Bonaparte;* as benefactors of mankind, like *Albert Schweitzer*, or *Henry Dunant;* as religious founders, like *Mohammed*, or *Buddha;* as poets, like *Shakespeare*, or *Goethe;* as inventors, like *Gutenberg*, or *Edison;* as exponents of evolution, like *Darwin*, or *Haeckel;* or as preachers of the Gospel, like *Spurgeon*, or *Billy Graham.*

It was never ever prophesied about any one of these, or indeed any other persons, that they would one day arise and stand out on account of this or that deed or action. God did not even announce in advance the coming of individual prophets who would faithfully proclaim His word. Not one of the biographies of their lives was made known beforehand. No-one knew 400 years before he was born that the Holy Roman Emperor *Charlemagne* would walk on this earth, and no-one predicted that *Mohammed* would come.

There is only one person in all of world history of whose life story and conduct, at the time of His appearing on the world stage, we have precisely-foretold details. There is only one person concerning whom the place of His birth, His nature and works, and the circumstances and details surrounding His death were foretold—and even set in a written record—centuries before His birth. These details were incrementally disclosed, over several centuries, bit by bit; and they were refined and made more precise with the addition of supplementary details. As a result, a biography of sorts was developed that was so specific that it could only refer to one particular person. Very significantly, the documents were known to the public centuries before His appearing. This situation, unique in world history, applies to only one single person, and that is **Jesus Christ**.

How is something like this possible? Only the divine omniscience of the God of the Bible could foresee it, and nothing other than His omnipotence could also— when the fullness of time had come (Galatians 4:4) — transpose it point for point into reality.

In the foregoing story, rendered in such detail, Solomon explained many words of prophecy to the Queen of Sheba which referred to the coming Messiah. In the New Testament, all the references to the Messiah were precisely fulfilled in Jesus. Only He alone could therefore say, with reference to the Old Testament: "You search the Scriptures … and it is they that bear witness of me" (John 5:39). No-one else could fulfil this claim, which is why no false Christ could ever appeal to fulfilled prophecy to prove his claims. Only Jesus could say: "Moses wrote of me" (John 5:46) and "Abraham saw my day" (John 8:56).

The life of Jesus as attested to in the New Testament was unique. It transpired exactly according to the divine plan which had been prophesied in the Old Testament. He was the One sent by God, who fulfilled the will of the Father; the One who accomplished the task of Redeemer, and fulfilled all the prophecies made about Him:

> "And we have seen and testify that the Father has sent His Son to be the Savior of the world".
>
> (1 John 4:14)

> "Behold, I have come to do your will, O God, as it is written of me in the scroll of the book".
>
> (Hebrews 10:7)

Through a series of New Testament statements we will now show how the prophetic promises concerning the Messiah came to be fulfilled in Jesus.

The birthplace of the Messiah

According to Micah 5:1, the Messiah was to be born in Bethlehem. In Jesus' lifetime, this village was a place with fewer than 1,000 inhabitants. Until shortly before the time for Jesus to be born, Mary lived in the wrong place, if her child was to be the Messiah. Only the order of the Emperor *Augustus*, concerning the taking of the census, meant that Mary, well advanced in her pregnancy, came to be in Bethlehem:

"And Joseph also went up from Galilee, from the town of Nazareth, to Judea, to the city of David, which is called Bethlehem, because he was of the lineage of David" (Luke 2:4).

"And while they were there, the time came for her to give birth. And she gave birth to her firstborn son" (Luke 2:6–7a).

The messianic line of descent

The line of descent of the Messiah that had been revealed in the Old Testament (OT) bit by bit over several centuries is unfolded and outlined in detail in the New Testament in two places.

The *one family tree* is that of Mary, the mother of Jesus. Here we will select several members out of the family tree contained in the Gospel of Luke (Luke 3:23–38), which extends from Mary's father right back to Adam: Eli—Matthat—Levi- … -Melea—Menna—Mattatha—Nathan—David—Jesse—Obed—Boaz—Salmon- … -Hezron—Perez—Judah—Jacob—Isaac—Abraham—Terah—Nahor—Serug—Reu—Peleg—Eber—Shelah—Cainan—Arphaxad—Shem—Noah—Lamech—Methuselah—Enoch—Jared—Mahalaleel—Cainan—Enos—Seth—Adam.

The *other family tree* can be found in the Gospel of Matthew (Matthew 1:1–17), beginning with Abraham and ending with Joseph, the husband of Mary: Abraham—

Isaac—Jacob—Judah—Perez—Hezron- … -Salmon—Boaz –Obed—Jesse—David—Solomon—Rehoboam—Abijah—Asaph—Jehoshaphat—Joram- Uzziah—Jotham—Ahaz—Hezekiah- … - Eliud—Eleazar—Matthan—Jacob—Joseph. Verse 16, "Jacob the father of Joseph the husband of Mary, of whom Jesus was born, who is called Christ", draws attention to the fact that while Joseph is a direct descendant of David, it is nevertheless not through Joseph that Jesus was to come "from David's body".[18] That took place through Mary, who was also a direct descendant of David.

Jesus is the Messiah

In the synagogue at Nazareth Jesus read out the prophecy from Isaiah 61:1–2, which refers to the Messiah. As the eyes of everyone present were fixed on Him, He attested to them: "Today this Scripture has been fulfilled in your hearing" (Luke 4:21), and with that He declared Himself to be the Messiah.

The conversation of Jesus that is recorded in the New Testament in the most detail took place with the Samaritan woman at Jacob's Well. She knew about the coming of the Messiah: "I know that Messiah is coming (he who is called Christ).[19] When he comes, he will tell

---

[18] 2 Samuel 7:12–"When your days are fulfilled and you lie down with your fathers, I will raise up your offspring after you, who shall come *from your body*, and I will establish His kingdom."

[19] Christ describes the office of Jesus. The Greek word *christos* is the translation of the Aramaic word *meschicha* and the Hebrew word *maschiach,* which means Messiah.

us all things" (John 4:25). She did not anticipate Jesus' answer: "I who speak to you am he" (John 4:26).

The Messiah is not the Saviour for Israel alone, but also for the Gentiles

Jesus restored sight to the blind, caused the lame to walk, the mute to speak, and raised the dead to life. This was an expression of His love and compassion, and yet it was ultimately only a side-effect of His mission. His main commission, in leaving Heaven and coming down to us humans, was to save us from being eternally lost: "For the Son of Man came to seek and to save the lost" (Luke 19:10). Many other references testify to the fact that Jesus is the Saviour:

> "I came not to call the righteous, but sinners"
> (Matthew 9:13)

> "For God did not send His Son into the world to condemn the world, but in order that the world might be saved through Him. Whoever believes in Him is not condemned" (John 3:17–18).

Even in the Old Testament the Messiah is already foretold to be the Saviour of the Gentiles. After His resurrection Jesus gives His disciples the famous command for global evangelism, known as the Great Commission:

"Go therefore and make disciples of all nations, baptizing them in the name of the Father and of the Son and of the Holy Spirit, teaching them to observe all that I have commanded you" (Matthew 28:19–20).

After the conversion of Paul, the risen Jesus said to Ananias, who blessed and baptised him: "He is a chosen instrument of mine to carry my name before the Gentiles and kings and the children of Israel" (Acts 9:15).

The Messiah is king of an eternal kingdom

Daniel 7:14 declares the Messiah to be the king of an eternal kingdom. Jesus also attests to this before Pilate: "My kingdom is not from the world" (John 18:36). Whereupon Pilate asked: "'So you are a king?' Jesus answered, 'You say that I am a king'" (John 18:37). The wise men from the East looked for the "newborn king" (Matthew 2:2) and found Him as a baby in the manger. The Messiah is God, and is also the Creator.

The Jews wanted to kill Jesus for two reasons; because He broke the Sabbath, and because He "was even calling God His own Father, making Himself equal with God" (John 5:18).Even though the Jews rejected Him, they nevertheless recognised His claim to be God.

Furthermore we can look at two texts from the Psalms, which give the impression that here the reference is to God the Father:

"Your throne, O God, is forever and ever. The sceptre of your kingdom is a sceptre of uprightness; you have loved righteousness and hated wickedness. Therefore God, your God, has anointed you with the oil of gladness beyond your companions" (Psalm 45:6–7).

"O my God, … take me not away in the midst of my days … Of old you laid the foundation of the earth, and the heavens are the work of your hands" (Psalm 102:24–25).

These two texts from the Psalms are then quoted in the New Testament in the first chapter of the letter to the Hebrews. This entire chapter speaks exclusively about the Son of God, and we read:

"Of the Son he says [and now Psalm 45:6–7 is quoted]: 'Your throne, O God, is forever and ever, the sceptre of uprightness is the sceptre of your kingdom. You have loved righteousness and hated wickedness; therefore God, your God, has anointed you with the oil of gladness beyond your companions.'" (Hebrews 1:8–9).

"And, 'You, Lord, laid the foundation of the earth in the beginning, and the heavens are the work of your hands" (Hebrews 1:10, quoting Psalm 102:25).

It is thus clearly stated that Jesus is God, and Jesus is also the Creator. The heavens are the work of His hands! Other New Testament texts declare the Lord Jesus to be the Creator of all things:

> "In the beginning was the Word, and the Word was with God, and the Word was God … All things were made through him, and without him was not anything made that was made" (John 1:1 & 3).

If we decipher this text with the help of the following verses 10 and 14 of the same chapter, then we can also write:

> In the beginning was Jesus, and Jesus was with God, and Jesus was God. All things were made through Jesus, and without Jesus was not anything made that was made.

It is written just as clearly in Colossians 1:15–17:

> "He (= Jesus) is the image of the invisible God, the firstborn of all creation. For by him (= Jesus) all things were created, in heaven and on earth, visible and invisible, whether thrones or dominions or rulers or authorities—all things were created through him and for him. And he is before all things, and in him all things hold together."

We can never think highly enough of Jesus, for His work in creation extends not only to the micro-cosmos with its atomic structures, but it reaches far beyond our macro-cosmos with all its countless galaxies. By His authoritative word He also called into existence the for-us-as-yet-invisible realm of God. He alone could say "I am the life" (John 14:6), and that is why He is also the source of all earthly life.

The Messiah as teacher

No-one has ever preached as authoritatively and as profoundly as Jesus. The Sermon on the Mount (Matthew 5–7) is the most powerful teaching ever presented to humanity. From Mark 1:22 we learn what effect His sermons had: "And they were astonished at his teaching, for he taught them as one who had authority, and not as the scribes."

The character of the Messiah

Jesus was the only teacher who ever walked this earth and Himself did all that He taught. Such a concept is not to be found in religion. No religious founder has ever fulfilled what He has taught others. In this, Jesus is unique. Some examples of this:

Fulfilling the Law: The people of the Old Covenant were taught to keep God's Law. Not one person has ever been able to fulfil the law—but Jesus did (Galatians 4:4–5).

Empathy in joy and sorrow: In Romans 12:15 the Bible teaches: "Rejoice with those who rejoice, weep with those who weep." At the wedding at Cana, Jesus celebrated with the happy wedding guests. But when Lazarus had died and He saw how Mary, and also the Jews, were crying (John 11:33ff.), Jesus also cried with them, even though He knew that within minutes He would be raising him to life again.

Always forgiving: In Matthew 18:21 Peter asked the Lord: "How often will my brother sin against me, and I forgive Him? As many as seven times?" To which Jesus replied in Matthew 18:22: "I do not say to you seven times, but seventy times seven." Jesus meant by this: not only 490 times, but always! This saying of Jesus is very encouraging for us. If Jesus requires of us that we always forgive, then we can be certain that He Himself will most definitely act this way toward us.

This characteristic feature of Jesus, to love people coming out of every situation and to accept them, is amply demonstrated for us in the New Testament:

> "Come to me, all who labor and are heavy laden, and I will give you rest. Take my yoke upon you, and learn from me, for I am gentle and lowly in heart, and you will find rest for your souls" (Matthew 11:28–29).

> "I am the good shepherd. The good shepherd lays down his life for the sheep" (John 10:11).

> "My sheep hear my voice, and I know them, and they follow me. I give them eternal life, and they

will never perish, and no one will snatch them out of my hand" (John 10:27–28).

"This is my commandment, that you love one another as I have loved you. Greater love has no one than this, that someone lays down his life for his friends" (John 15:12–13).

The Messiah is the only one without sin

Jesus was the only one to walk on this earth without ever sinning. But He was *"in every respect … tempted as we are, yet without sin"* (Hebrews 4:15).

The various apostles highlighted His sinlessness in line with their individual personalities:

John was the apostle who valued the love of his Lord more than the others. His thinking was characterized by much thoughtfulness and depth. It is thus understandable that this apostle describes sin as something totally foreign to Jesus' nature: *"In him there is no sin"* (1 John 3:5).

Peter, the outspoken fisherman from Galilee, shows himself again and again to be a man of action. It is therefore fitting that he attests to Jesus' sinlessness from the perspective of His actions: *"He committed no sin"* (1 Peter 2:22).

Paul was an educated man who had studied under the (at that time) world-renowned professorship of Gamaliel (Acts 22:3). Thus, knowledge was particularly significant for him, and thus he speaks of Jesus as of *"Him… who knew no sin"* (2 Corinthians 5:21).

The Messiah as healer of illnesses

In the synagogue of Nazareth Jesus reads (Luke 4:17–19) the text from Isaiah 61:1–2 and applies this text to Himself: *"He (= God) has sent me to proclaim liberty to the captives and recovering of sight to the blind, to set at liberty those who are oppressed."* The New Testament records in detail how appropriately this passage fitted Him. Wherever Jesus went, people with all kinds of ailments promptly appeared. For Him there was no such thing as an unhealable case, because Matthew 4:23 declares: "And he (= Jesus) went throughout all Galilee, teaching in their synagogues and proclaiming the Gospel of the kingdom and healing **every** disease and **every** affliction among the people."

The death of the Messiah

Even in the face of death Jesus remained the one in control. In His appearances before the High Priest in Israel and Pilate, the Roman governor, He affirmed what He had earlier claimed (John 10:18): "No one takes it [my life] from me, but I lay it down of my own accord. I have authority to lay it down, and I have authority to take it up again. This charge I have received from my Father." With His declaration on the cross, "It is finished" (John 19:30), the victory was won over hell, death and the devil. In Luke 23:46 we read: "Then Jesus, calling out with a loud voice, said, 'Father, into your hands I commit my spirit!' And having said this he breathed his last." With that, the final stroke of the work of salvation was accomplished. The cross, this unimaginably gruesome Roman method of execution, became by the will of God the sign of salvation for a lost world.

The resurrection of the Messiah

Jesus did not remain in the grave—He rose from the dead! The resurrection of Jesus is the most significant fact in the entire history of the world. It had never before occurred that someone had risen permanently from the dead. Jesus is the only one:

> "But on the first day of the week, at early dawn, they [= the women] went to the tomb … And they found the stone rolled away from the tomb, but when they went in they did not find the body of the Lord Jesus. While they were perplexed about this, behold, two men stood by them in dazzling apparel … the men said to them, 'Why do you seek the living among the dead? He is not here, but has risen.'" (Luke 24:1–6).

The huge significance of the Resurrection is presented in 1 Corinthians 15:17–20:

"And if Christ has not been raised, your faith is futile and you are still in your sins. Then those also who have fallen asleep in Christ have perished. If in this life only we have hope in Christ, we are of all people most to be pitied. But in fact Christ has been raised from the dead, the firstfruits of those who have fallen asleep."

The Second Coming of the Messiah

In Daniel 7:13–14 the mightiest event the world will ever witness is prophetically foreseen. It is the return of the Messiah:

'I saw in the night visions, and behold, with the clouds of heaven there came one like a son of man, and he came to the Ancient of Days and was presented before him. And to him was given dominion and glory and a kingdom, that all peoples, nations, and languages should serve him; His dominion is an everlasting dominion, which shall not pass away, and his kingdom one that shall not be destroyed.'

That day will be the greatest future event in world history. We are rapidly approaching this day, because in Daniel 12:7 it is written: "When the shattering [or 'scattering', Hebrew *naw-fats*] of the power of the holy people comes to an end all these things would be finished." Many commentators over the centuries have seen this as the time when the Jews ceased from being dispersed and returned to their nation. For example, the *John Gill* wrote in the 1700s in his famous commentary that this could well refer to "the Jews; when the dispersion of them, who were formerly a holy people to the Lord, and shall be so again, will be over." He foresaw this coming "return to their own land", i.e. Israel, as associated with a mass national conversion, which would therefore be yet to come.

In Gill's time, the idea of the restoration of the Jewish homeland would have been regarded as fanciful. Yet, since 1948, there has once again been a State of Israel. With that, God has turned the hand of the world clock to just before midnight. In Matthew 24:30 Jesus Himself clearly foretold His return:

> "Then will appear in heaven the sign of the Son of Man, and then all the tribes of the earth will mourn, and they will see the Son of Man coming in the clouds of heaven with power and great glory."

Shouldn't this day be a huge reason for joy for the whole of humanity? The Creator of the world appearing in person! The Saviour of the world is coming! But why is it written in the Book of Revelation 1:7: "All tribes of the earth will wail on account of Him"? Why do the people concerned call out to the rocks and mountains: "Fall on us and hide us from [his] face" (Revelation 6:16)? Most people traverse paths where Jesus does not feature at all, or merely on the periphery. Renowned atheists write bestsellers that try to explain God away. Evolutionary theorists imagine they need no intelligent author for the unimaginable quantity of information in every living cell. But on that day God will become visible reality. All deniers of God and agnostics and all Bible critics—even if they appeared in holy garb—will now recognize the error of their ways. Now they are lost, and can no longer revise anything; it's finally too late. That is why they cry and mourn.

Everyone will see Jesus, the Messiah: "Behold, he is coming with the clouds, and every eye will see him, even those who pierced him, and all tribes of the earth will wail on account of him", writes John in Revelation 1:7. When on 21 July 1969 *Neil Armstrong* was the first man to set foot on the moon, 500 million people followed this event via television. *Lady Diana* of England lost her life in a motor vehicle accident. When her funeral took place in London on 6 September 1997, it made history as the first 'global funeral'. 2.5 billion people followed the event on television—40 percent of the world population at the time! This figure has not been surpassed for any event since. But no television camera will be required to broadcast the coming of Jesus. All people will witness this greatest event in world history 'live'; Jesus will be visible to everyone. That not only applies to the world population alive at the time, but to all generations in the history of humanity. Then only one question will remain for discussion: Do I belong in the number of the saved, or among the lost? For the saved, that which was prophetically foreseen by Malachi will be true:

"But for you who fear my name, the sun of righteousness shall rise with healing in its wings. You shall go out leaping like calves from the stall" (Malachi 4:2).

Jesus is this sun of righteousness. With that the end of world history has arrived. For some it will signal the beginning of endless joyful celebration, while for all others it will forever be too late.

Epilogue—Part I:

Retrospective

You have now read the interesting story, 'I wasn't told the half of it'. It dealt with the journey of the Queen of Sheba, from the perspective of that time in history. We trust it gave you not just pleasure but held your interest to the end. In my experience, this story of the journey recorded in 2 Chronicles 9:1–9 & 12 is seldom the subject of preaching. It is however an engaging and fascinating occurrence, worthy of detailed attention, as has now taken place in this book. In a lively way, *Jasmin Yildiz* took us back into this story of a journey that took place about 3000 years ago, teasing out for our imagination in great detail how everything could have transpired. In an imaginative way she augments the story by also telling us about the childhood of the queen, who often tested the patience of her story-telling grandmother by her pointed questions. Her alert mind justifiably questions the making of sacrifices to gods who have never shown themselves to, nor spoken with, people, and who have never given people a complete framework for living. When she first hears of the wise King Solomon after her coronation, she soon sets out on an arduous journey through the desert to seek answers to her questions. In conversations spread over many days she learns of the true God, who alone has communicated with mankind by the spoken word. What she can hardly believe are the prophetic utterances about the coming Messiah. *Jasmin Yildiz* has masterfully gathered all the key Old Testament references to the Messiah, presenting them vividly in the form of interesting dialogues between Solomon and the Queen of Sheba. Eventually this royal traveller from afar also turns to the living God, after having her searching questions answered.

This book was not written to add another volume to the mass of entertainment literature. With reference to such books, Solomon, even in his day, said: "Of making many books there is no end" (Ecclesiastes 12:12). Our intent is very specific and targeted. It is to provide, for people who have not as yet found the only true God, a practical aid to doing just that. Who would be better equipped than the heathen Queen of Sheba, who brought no Bible knowledge of any kind with her, to take on the role of the questioning seeker? Anyone who is truly seeking after God can recognize themselves in this person with her alert mind and her many questions.

God can be found in the Messiah He has sent, and that is Jesus Christ. That is why a sermon about the Queen of Sheba has been attached to this story of a journey, a sermon that illuminates the event from a New Testament perspective. In the New Testament we come face to face with the Messiah who by then has already come, and who is the only door to the Kingdom of Heaven. So the third part of the epilogue is titled: 'How can I get to Heaven?' May there be many readers who accept God's loving offer in Jesus Christ, and so find eternal life.

Epilogue—Part II:

The Queen of Sheba's journey—from a New Testament perspective.

Introduction

In the Bible we encounter four prominent travel stories about foreigners who, after elaborate preparations for their journey, came to Israel. Two of these accounts are in the New Testament, and two in the Old.

Matthew 2:1–12: The **Wise Men from the East** came from Babylon. They were looking for the newborn king of the Jews. The indicator for their trip was a new star that had never been seen before. They followed the star and found Jesus, Israel's Messiah.

Acts 8:26–40: The **Finance Minister from Ethiopia** wanted to worship God in Jerusalem. Only on his return journey through the desert did he find God in Jesus, who became his Saviour.

2 Kings 5:1–17: The **Syrian Captain** was smitten with leprosy. He sought healing in Israel and found it after numerous detours. His source of information was a Jewish girl, who was a servant in the Captain's household.

2 Chronicles 9:1–12: The **Queen of Sheba** came from the south and wanted to see if Solomon was truly as wise as she had been told. She came in response to a rumour and was astonished at what she found.

What do these four travellers have in common?

- They all had to make laborious and extensive preparations for their trip.

- Not one of them had received an invitation from Israel. All travelled at their own prompting.

- With the exception of the Ethiopian Finance Minister, they all brought magnificent gifts with them.

- All four travellers not only found exactly what they had sought, but in some cases far more.

- All of the travellers found the true God.

At this point we will only focus on one of these four journeys, that of **the Queen of Sheba.** The text is found in 2 Chronicles 9:1–9 & 12 (parallel text reference: 1 Kings 10:1–13).

Rolf Beyer, a freelance author and high school teacher, has written a book of over 300 pages titled 'The Queen of Sheba'.[20] The length of this volume is especially re-markable, given that the only source of information about this queen is the Bible, where we have a mere twelve verses. On the back cover, *Beyer* writes:

---

[20] *Rolf Beyer*: The Queen of Sheba, Albatross Publishers, Düsseldorf, 1987, 304 p. (German)

"She is one of the most well-known figures of world history, and yet no-one knows who she really was. The mysterious queen from the legend-surrounded kingdom of the Sabaeans has for almost 3000 years lived on in various cultures, in Jewish legend as in Islamic mythology."

Some examples to demonstrate this:

Novels have been written about her (*J. Dos Passos:* Three Soldiers. New York 1932; *R. Kipling:* The Butterfly That Stamped; *Ph. A. Crutch:* The Queen of Sheba. Her Life and Times. 1922; *A. Colin-Simard:* Au Nome la Reine de Saba. Paris 1986).

Composers have been inspired by her to write music (*G. F. Handel:* Solomon, 1749; *Ch. Gounod:* La Reine de Saba, 1862; *K. Goldmark:* The Queen of Sheba, 1875). **Movies** about her have been filmed (e.g., Taurus Film, La Reine de Saba, Munich 1975 with the Italian Actress *Gina Lollobridgida*).

Beyer writes: "The fascinating, almost three-thousand-year-old story of the Queen of Sheba is at first glance a brittle and terse account, which raises more questions than it offers facts. It deals with the visit of the queen to Solomon, and to this day is the only ancient source that speaks of her."

That all sounds as though the text were not much use. And it certainly does raise a string of unanswered questions:

The queen's name is not mentioned at all. The fact that she remains nameless is remarkable, since names in the Bible repeatedly play a significant role. Even name changes after particular encounters with God are clearly emphasised:

- A Jacob became an Israel
- An Abram became Abraham
- A Peter became Cephas, a rock.

The question as to what language the king and queen conversed in also remains unanswered.

The queen's country of origin remains just as much a mystery as the route she travelled on her journey.

We're not even told the questions with which the queen quizzed Solomon, let alone his answers. Subsequent storytellers have thus gone ahead and invented riddles of their choosing.

So, after these critical observations, how might we arrive at an understanding of this biblical passage?

1. A state visit

We first note that the Old Testament here describes a state visit. In our day, too, we frequently hear reports in the media of the heads of state of various countries paying each other visits. These include:

- *Visits of friendship,* intended to consolidate and strengthen relations with another country.

- Or possibly a *working visit,* to sort out unresolved economic issues or discuss mutual problems.

- Or we could picture the *G8 Summit* of 6–8 June 2007, at which eight heads of state met together in Heiligendamm on the Baltic Sea, to consider world problems. An extra-large canopied beach chair was even manufactured, with room enough for all eight of this world's great ones. Journalists' photographs of these heads of state garnered global attention.

I too, once witnessed the state visit of a queen, though only as a bystander, so to speak. It was in the 1960s, when *Queen Elizabeth II* paid a visit to the Federal Republic of Germany. I was still a student in Hannover at the time. It was widely known that the queen would be travelling in her Rolls Royce on Saturday night at eight o'clock along the Herrenhäuser Avenue, to a reception in her honour at the Palace Herrenhausen. People lined the avenue for many hours beforehand, in order to catch even a short glimpse of her as she passed by.

The visit of the Queen of Sheba with Solomon was entirely different. There was no protocol to regulate every minute of the visit. There were also no economic discussions, nor deliberations that would finally lead to a mutually acceptable treaty.

For instance, Solomon had not sent a written invitation via couriers to the queen. No, the Queen of Sheba set out on her own initiative. She acted entirely on the basis of rumour.

News about Solomon's renown, particularly of his great wisdom, had reached her ears. She could have remained at home, but she decided on a strenuous and lengthy journey through the desert. She set off to Jerusalem with a huge entourage. It was no rapid and comfortable flight with a modern airline, but rather an arduous journey by camel caravan. We can easily reckon with a travel time of around six weeks. Whatever was it that drove her to make preparations for such a costly trip, and then to roam across the desert for weeks on end through sandstorms and great heat?

2. The reason for the journey

The Queen of Sheba wanted to test Solomon's wisdom, and so she brought with her a number of questions and riddles. Then the text states (vv. 1 & 2):

> *"And when she came to Solomon, she told him all that was on her mind. And Solomon answered all her questions."*

Unfortunately the questions the queen put to Solomon have not been recorded for us. We would very much have wanted to know more. Human imagination sees this as a challenge, and so numerous speculations exist. One collection of Jewish sermons of the 10th or 11th century—the *Midrash Mishle*—contains a number of riddles. These were, however, subsequent inventions.

3. The wisdom of Solomon

In the book of Kings we are told how God blessed Solomon richly with wisdom:

> *"And God gave Solomon wisdom and understanding beyond measure, and breadth of mind like the sand on the seashore, so that Solomon's wisdom surpassed the wisdom of all the people"*
>
> *(1 Kings 4:29 & 30).*

We are further told that he wrote 3000 proverbs and more than 1000 songs (1 Kings 4:32), only a fraction of which have been handed down to us in the Book of Proverbs, the Song of Solomon and Ecclesiastes. Here we see how God gives in abundance when He is asked for something. Had the 'Guinness Book of Records' already existed in His day, Solomon would have been certain of holding the record in the category of wisdom.

The Queen of Sheba had come to witness and test the wisdom of Solomon. We need first to ask ourselves what wisdom is.

What is wisdom?

- Was it wisdom that enabled the Egyptians to build the pyramids?

- Was it wisdom that allowed the Greeks in antiquity to develop their philosophy?

- Was it wisdom when *Karl Marx* said: "Religion is the opiate of the people"?

- Is it wisdom that makes it possible for us to fly to the moon?

- Is it wisdom, when biologists today proudly claim to be close to being able to create life?

- Was it wisdom, when *Kant* and *Lessing* formulated their enlightening ideas?

- Was it wisdom, with which *Lessing* wrote the Parable of the Ring, in which he intended to say that it is surely entirely irrelevant which religion one follows?

- Is it wisdom, when modern theologians pick apart the Bible, so that one has more faith in the Bible critique than in the Bible itself?

The Bible teaches us that wisdom has a source, and that particular source is Jesus:

"In [Christ] are hidden all the treasures of wisdom and knowledge" (Colossians 2:3).

The achievements in the above list required much intelligence, but they all occurred without Christ. They therefore all without exception represent something solely thought out by humans. All thoughts and attitudes, on the other hand, with which we can orient our lives aright for eternity, can be defined as wisdom. They are those thoughts and attitudes which have Christ as their original cause and are therefore in harmony with Him. That enables us to recognize the clear distinction between intelligence and wisdom.

That brings us to a fundamental question:

4. How may we interpret the journey of the Queen of Sheba?

Attempting to find out what the riddles of the queen may have been does not get at the heart of the biblical message. In my search for the key to this story of a journey I came across John 5:39. There Jesus says:

> **"You search the Scriptures because you think that in them you have eternal life; and it is they that bear witness about me."**

When Jesus spoke about the Scriptures, He was referring to the Old Testament (OT), because at that time the New Testament (NT) had not even been written yet. So we are faced with the task of teasing out from the texts of the OT, again and again, *where* and *how* in any given place the reference is to Jesus, and in which way the subject of eternal life is being addressed there. This means for us that the right approach to the story about the journey will only have been found when we have discovered Jesus in it, and recognized how it points to eternal life.

For a given event recorded in the OT, the NT only very rarely hands us directly the interpretation that points to Jesus. In most cases, we need to work it out for ourselves, by reading the text from the perspective of the NT.

Example: When the people of Israel suffered a lack of water during their wandering in the wilderness, God told Moses to strike the rock (Exodus 17:6). In the NT, in 1 Corinthians 10:4, the rock that was struck is interpreted as referring to Jesus:

> *"They drank from the spiritual Rock that followed them, and the Rock was Christ."*

Here we learn something very remarkable: The OT text speaks about a very ordinary issue, namely how during wanderings in the wilderness a lack of water arises. And God offers a solution, in that Moses is to *strike* the rock. Who would even guess here that this text speaks of Jesus?

In a subsequent situation in the desert there is another shortage of water. Moses turns to God and asks for help. This time God says to Moses:

> *"Speak to the rock!"* (Numbers 20:8).

Moses probably thought, I've had good results by striking, and so he struck the rock once more. But that was our unholy human striving to give God's promises a helping hand. It was therefore disobedience, with the result that Moses was only permitted to view the Promised Land from afar, but could not enter it.

What was God telling us in this story? The rock here is a picture of Jesus. He is only 'struck' one single time for sin (on the cross of Calvary); now one is to speak to Jesus about sin. God wanted to make this principle plain by using the picture of the occurrence in the wilderness. And Moses arbitrarily destroyed this meaning.

The story of the journey: Who or what in this travel story of the Queen of Sheba points to Jesus? If Solomon is described as the wisest of all human beings (1 Kings 5:11) and Jesus as the source of wisdom (Colossians 2:3), it becomes obvious to see Jesus in Solomon.

Why, do we think, are we not given the name of the queen? Why not give the name of her country of origin, or the language she spoke? I suggest for this reason, that we can now put our own name in its place—irrespective of what land we are from, or what language we speak.

From now on, we will look at this travel story by identifying Solomon with Jesus; and we all—whether man or woman—are as of this instant the Queen of Sheba. That applies not only to the timeframe of the present sermon; we can retain this promotion to the Queen of Sheba for the rest of our lives! With this perspective in mind, we will now examine several of the statements in the text:

The king gave everything

> *"King Solomon gave to the Queen of Sheba all that she desired."* (2 Chronicles 9:12).

Does not Jesus do exactly the same for us? In John 15:7 we are given an equally far-reaching promise, which also contains the idea of **all:**

> *"If you abide in me, and my words abide in you, ask whatever you wish, and it will be done for you."*

The Gospel of Mark (chap. 9:22b-23) contains the account of a boy possessed by an evil spirit. His father comes to Jesus and says:

> *"'But if you can do anything, have compassion on us and help us'. And Jesus said to him, 'If you can! All things are possible for one who believes'."*

Are all things truly possible for God? To illustrate, let me tell a truly incredible story:

In Siberia: Recently, I heard from my Swiss Gideon-friend *Paul Koch* a remarkable story that took place in Siberia. In a certain village there lived a professing atheist. Sometimes, however, he was not quite so certain about his atheism. One day, as he was travelling through the Taiga (snowforest), He came into a large clearing, where he asked himself whether there is a God. There, in the solitude, all alone, He yelled loudly into the forest: "God, I want to know if you even exist! If YES, then show me, but please at once!" He had just uttered the sentence, when a book fell from the sky—directly at his feet. He was rather astonished, yes, even frightened, by this prompt response and picked up the book, on which was written in Russian "Biblja". He ran back to the village with the book and told the villagers the wonderful story. The strange book was passed from hand to hand, and the people read in the book that fell from the sky. At this point, what Jesus said, happened: "You search the Scriptures, and you will find me in them." It became known that 30 people came to faith through this Bible, among them the man in the Taiga.

An angel from heaven: Of course God could throw a Bible from heaven—fresh off the *heavenly presses,* so to speak. Even now, during this sermon, God could have sent an angel from heaven, to tell us the Gospel. Such a messenger, who has just come from seeing God face-to-face, could do this far better, with more authority and authenticity, than we in our weakness can attempt to do it. But often it is God's intention to do His work in this world through us humans. In Noah's day, God could have created an ark in the blink of an eye, but He used Noah to construct the rescue vessel, even though it took him many decades.

So then, how did God do this in Siberia? A helicopter was flying over this Siberian territory with aid packages from the West on board. In the helicopter a Russian was searching through the cartons. He accepted clothing and food items. But when he found the carton of Bibles, he tossed the contents out of the helicopter with the words: "We don't need something like this here in Russia." One of those books fell directly at the feet of this very man.

Isn't that powerful, how God brought all that together? Precise timing combined with drop-off location accuracy to the centimetre. We know of many attributes of God; now we can add yet another: God can aim well, too!

b) On the throne of David

In verse 8 the queen says:

> *"Blessed be the LORD your God, who has delighted in you and set you on his throne as king for the LORD your God!"*

Curious that this pagan queen should utter a very apt description, which points to the kingship of Jesus. It is in line with what we read in Hebrews 1:8–9 about Jesus:

"But of the Son he (God) says, [Psalm 45:7–8] 'Your throne, O God, is forever and ever, the sceptre of uprightness is the sceptre of your kingdom. You have loved righteousness and hated wickedness; therefore God, your God, has anointed you with the oil of gladness beyond your companions."

In Isaiah 9:6–7 we have a further notable reference in relation to the throne of Jesus:

"For to us a child is born, to us a son is given; and the government shall be upon his shoulder, … of the increase of his government and of peace there will be no end, on the throne of David and over his kingdom, to establish it and to uphold it with justice and with righteousness from this time forth and forevermore."

Further, it is written in Jeremiah 33:17:

"For thus says the Lord: *'David shall never (so, not in eternity either) lack a man to sit on the throne of the house of Israel.'"*

Solomon is the *first king* after David. Jesus is the *last and the eternal king.*

c) The king answered every question

"And Solomon answered all her questions"
(2 Chronicles 9:2).

We pass through this life with a multitude of unanswered questions. These are questions concerning God, and questions that affect us very personally or that relate to the people in our immediate circle:

- We do not understand why Job had to bear such immeasurable suffering, even though he was "blameless and upright, one who feared God and turned away from evil" (Job 1:1). In all the 42 chapters of the Book of Job we are not given any explanation. On the contrary: God puts 77 questions about creation to Job, who cannot answer even a single one of them:
  - Who is the father of the rain?
  - Who originated the drops of the dew?
  - Can you bind the chains of the Pleiades?
  - Who provides the raven with its food?

- We do not understand either, why the devil still had access to heaven after his fall, and even received permission from God to torment Job so unimaginably. Should he not have been confined to hell long ago?

- Nor do we understand why a man like *Hitler* was permitted to run Germany into the ground and trigger a World War, at the cost of a total of 50 million lives. Why did every one of the 39 documented attempts on his life fail (the unofficial figure is considerably higher)?

- I do not understand why my mother in East Prussia was transported to the Ukraine in the Second World War and had to die after only a few weeks in a concentration camp.

- And so we could all add our own list of questions for which we do not have an answer.

One thing, however, is certain: Just as Solomon gave the Queen of Sheba an answer to all of her questions, so our King Jesus will give us a clear answer to all of our questions. That will take place when we arrive in the presence of our King. Then we will be like Him and see Him as He is (1 John 3:2), and at this sight all our questions will instantly be answered—nothing will remain of them and we will worship Him with indescribable joy!

Referring to their questions at the time, He promised His disciples:

"In that day you will ask nothing of me" (John 16:23).

And with that, Jesus was referring to Heaven. Notice the similarity with verse 2 of our text: *And Solomon answered all her questions.*

d) Gifts for the king

> *"Then she gave the king 120 talents of gold, and a very great quantity of spices, and precious stones"*
> (2 Chronicles 9:9).

Solomon was a very wealthy king. Would we be able to see his stockpile of gold and precious clothes, it would take our breath away. It is hard to grasp—the queen brings this so-very-wealthy-already king even more gold for his storehouses. 120 talents, that's 6000 kilograms or 120,000 gold bars each at 50 grams—as they are common today in trading banks.

With this, Jesus is teaching us, as His followers, not to arrive at our destination empty-handed. He does not expect gold or silver from us. The most valuable thing we can bring our King is 'fruit'. He does not look for the successes of our life, but the fruit:

> "I chose you and appointed you that you should go and bear fruit and that your fruit should abide" (John 15:16).

In the Sermon on the Mount Jesus says:

> "But lay up for yourselves treasures in heaven" (Matthew 6:20).

It is therefore a command of Jesus that we lay up treasures in heaven to be presented to Him on our arrival in heaven—just as the Queen of Sheba presented Solomon with her treasures. That is not being made righteous by works, but our expression of love and gratitude to our King. Children are often an example for us, with their directness, and cheerful behaviour. This story from Switzerland made a big impression on me:

The glass of water: A small girl could only just read in the Bible and found the saying of Jesus: *"And whoever gives one of these little ones even a cup of cold water … he will by no means lose his reward"* (Matthew 10:42). At which the girl went into the kitchen, filled a glass with water and ran with it out onto the street, in order to give it to someone. But at that moment there was no-one there, so she ran on to the edge of the forest. There she met a young man and offered him the glass with the words: "Drink this water in the name of Jesus!" He was totally astonished at this unusual happening. But because he just happened to be thirsty, he drank the water. The girl ran home with the empty glass and set it down in the kitchen.

Many years went by. In the meantime, the little girl had grown up and taken up a career in nursing. One day a man was admitted to her section of the hospital, and the first thing he did was to unpack his Bible and place it on his bedside table. Since this did not happen every day, the nurse asked the man if he was a believer. When he replied in the affirmative, she continued by asking him how he happened to come to faith. The man explained: "It was while I was still young. I saw no point to my life and made my way into the forest to take my life there. But at the edge of the forest a little girl with a glass of water came up to me and said: "Drink this in the name of Jesus!" That made such an impression on me that I held back from my intention, bought myself a Bible and came to faith very soon thereafter." To which the nurse said: "The little girl that day—that was me!"

By obeying only one single Bible verse, the little girl had won a soul for heaven. If Jesus turned water to wine at the wedding in Cana, then He will turn the water in that glass into gold in eternity. And that applies to all fruit that we bear in this life with God's help: the Lord will turn it to gold at our arrival in Heaven. These are the "treasures of heaven" of which Jesus spoke in the Sermon on the Mount.

Not that we want to leave the wrong impression: we cannot earn heaven with anything at all, Jesus won it for us at great cost on the cross.

e) Happy—to be with Jesus

> *"Happy are these your servants, who continually stand before you and hear your wisdom!"*
> (2 Chronicles 9:7).

The queen calls all those people happy, who can stand in Solomon's presence continually. By transposition this tells us: Happy are all those who will one day stand forever before King Jesus.

In Luke 12:47 those people are called blessed, who will be forever with Jesus:

> *"Blessed are those servants whom the master finds awake when he comes. Truly, I say to you, he will dress himself for service and have them recline at table, and he will come and serve them."*

f) The King gave over-generously

"And King Solomon gave to the Queen of Sheba all that she desired … besides what she had brought to the king" (2 Chronicles 9:12).

Whatever we may bring to our Lord, His gift to us will far surpass everything imaginable. In the terminology used in Luke 6:38, one can sense the inability of human language to describe the overflowing wealth of the gift of God:

"Good measure, pressed down, shaken together, running over, will be put into your lap."

Yes, our King Jesus gives us **everything**—the whole of Heaven!

g) Not even half was told me

"There was no more breath in her … . And she said to the king, 'The report was true that I heard in my own land of your words and of your wisdom, but I did not believe the reports until I came and my own eyes had seen it. And behold, half the greatness of your wisdom was not told me; you surpass the report that I heard'" (2 Chronicles 9:4–6).

The Queen of Sheba was speechless. The original Hebrew text says "there was no more life-breath" (Hebrew *ruach*) in her.

"And when the Queen of Sheba had seen the wisdom of Solomon … there was no more breath in her."

She was beside herself with astonishment. She could not have imagined anything like this. And because she could no longer contain herself, she had to tell Solomon. She admitted to him (2 Chronicles 9:5–6):

"The report was true that I heard in my own land of your words and of your wisdom, but I did not believe the reports until I came and my own eyes had seen it."

And then she uttered that thought (paraphrased here) that has deeply affected me personally:

I wasn't told the half of it!

No doubt we too will exclaim similarly, when we arrive in Jesus' presence. Not even half was told us, because at this time the glory of the Lord is still unimaginable for us. But in order to see Jesus' glory, we need to get up and go to Him—just as the Queen of Sheba once set out.

Only when we are with Him will we see Him "as He is". Then we won't believe our eyes, and we will stand before our Lord in amazement and declare: We did not anticipate the half of it.

When we get to Heaven we will say: How meagre were all our sermons (in comparison with what we will then see).

At this point in our lives we are still en route, like the Queen of Sheba once was, on her journey through the wilderness. She probably covered a distance of some 3000 kilometres with her caravan, since she came from the south.

- Perhaps she came from what today is Ethiopia
- Perhaps she came from the Arabian Peninsula;
- possibly from the land of the Sabaeans, today the land of Yemen.

The route through the desert would have been arduous, bringing with it many difficulties—but it was the way to the king. We, too, are still on the way to our king: our King Jesus Christ. We have not yet arrived in His presence, but we are on the path that leads us to our goal. This path often leads through the wilderness.

We can identify two different situations

1. Already on the way: Perhaps we have already been on the path toward our heavenly King Jesus for a long time. The Queen of Sheba was on her way to *Jerusalem.* As Christians we are still on the way, but we are on the way to the *heavenly Jerusalem.* At the time the king of the earthly Jerusalem was Solomon; the King of the heavenly Jerusalem is Jesus.

Our journey's route includes a long stretch through the wilderness. There are enemies, there is illness, and there are burdens. We Christians are no strangers to such things. The path through this world also leads us again and again through suffering and trials—through the wilderness, as it were. Therefore the words of the well-known hymn by *Zinzendorf*, 'Jesus, still lead on' are very fitting:

If the way be drear, if the foe be near, Let no faithless fears o'ertake us, Let not faith and hope forsake us, For through many a woe to our home we go.
The crucial thing is this: The way leads to Jesus, our King. That, too, was brought out in the last verse by *Zinzendorf*:

> *Jesus, still lead on, till our rest be won; Heavenly Leader, still direct us, Still support, control, protect us, Till we safely stand in our fatherland.*

In Matthew 12:42, Jesus said to the Pharisees:

> *"The queen of the South will rise up at the judgment with this generation and condemn it, for she came from the ends of the earth to hear the wisdom of Solomon, and behold, something greater than Solomon is here."*

Jesus compares Himself with Solomon: Here is something greater than Solomon!

If Solomon already gave reason for astonishment—and the queen was accustomed to wealth, or she would not have been able to bring gold in such great abundance with her—how much more will we one day stand before Jesus in amazement. That will be surprise and joy in the most perfect measure. The letter to the Corinthians gives us the correct perspective:

> "*What no eye has seen, nor ear heard, nor the heart of man imagined, what God has prepared for those who love Him*" (1 Corinthians 2:9).

2. Not as yet on the road: It may, however, be that we still live in the palace of our own worldview and comforts. If so, we are being called to leave the old habitation and set out with our caravan through the desert.

In the real desert, there are many dangers: snakes and scorpions and numerous wild animals; sandstorms and lack of water. The chariot can break down; even the camels can break down.

Just so, there are many different dangers and difficulties we can encounter on our way through the 'wilderness' to Jesus: We can become ill; there are many of life's circumstances which can bring us to despair. When we decide to follow Jesus, no 'Red Carpet' is rolled out, but we receive peace with God through the Blood of the Lamb, who graciously receives us. And now we go through life as His witnesses, led by His hand. The way will oftentimes be rough, but Jesus is with us.

But: The goal is incomparable! The goal is the eternal King! The goal is Heaven! Get up, on your feet, get moving; turn from any other way—because every path without Jesus leads into error, into eternal wilderness, into being eternally lost. Only the path with Jesus leads to the heavenly Jerusalem. Come and set out on this journey! To remain with the illustration—saddle up your camels this very day and set out on the journey; then you will have the greatest goal before you that was ever given to a person! Amen ... .

Epilogue—Part III:

How can I get into Heaven?

Is it worth unreservedly confessing my sins to Jesus and asking Him for forgiveness on the basis of His promise? Yes, because then He will, by grace, remove my sins from me and give me the gift of His righteousness. Otherwise, I will retain my sins. And these will in turn warrant God's just verdict for me—his eternal rejection, which is Hell.

Does it pay to place my entire life under the authority of Him who has given me everything?

Yes, because it's only in close relationship with Jesus, my Saviour and Lord, that my life can and will bear fruit to the glory of God. He is quite justified in looking for this from me, since I am, after all, supposed to be a credible pointer to the throne of His grace!

Unfortunately, the spirit of the age has moved into many churches, with the result that Hell is largely ignored. However, our life's path ends in a fork in the road, because God's holy demand must and will be fulfilled in eternity. It should be possible to find the indicators to this dividing of the ways, as well as the possibility of moving into one or other path, for or against Him, in every church. It is then also appropriate that **each** direction has an indicator that tells you where you will arrive.

For this reason, Jesus, in His sermons, not only attested to the existence of Hell, but also warned most urgently against it: *"If your right eye causes you to sin, tear it out and throw it away. For it is better that you lose one of your members than that your whole body be thrown into hell"* (Matthew 5:29). But Jesus came into this world with this express purpose: *'For the Son of Man came to seek and to save* (= for Heaven) *the lost'* (Luke 19:10). That means: If I confess my sin to Him and follow Him as my Lord and Saviour, He will give me peace with God and eternal life with HIM in Heaven. This abode is described in 1 Corinthians 2:9 as unimaginably beautiful: *"What no eye has seen, nor ear heard, nor the heart of man imagined, what God has prepared for those who love him."* The invitation stands! If you take it up, God will richly reward you.

Now we have arrived at the most important question of our lives, bar none: How can I be certain of getting into Heaven? Jesus has told us quite clearly: *"I am the door* (to Heaven)*"* (John 10:9) and *"I give them eternal life"* (John 10:28). Furthermore, He said: *"I am the way, and the truth, and the life. No one comes to the Father except through me"* (John 14:6). These words of Jesus, showing us the true way, simultaneously dismiss as worthless and misleading all paths offered in the various religions thought up by human imaginings. There is a very grave reason for this, shown in the following segment (*'The only way out'*). Only Christ, and He alone—no church, no human deeds, no religion—can get us into Heaven. This path will now be explained step by step, in the form of a dialogue. Should you wish to take this path, you can do so now, as if with the aid of a 'user manual', so to speak.

Recognize yourself in the light of the Bible: We read in Romans 3:22–23: *"For there is no distinction: for all have sinned and fall short of the glory of God."* This Bible text shows us our lost condition before the living God. Because of our sin, which separates us from God, we have no access to Him, and nothing to offer Him that could make us acceptable to Him. In short: We have no credit, but a massive debt before God, and we possess nothing that could reconcile us to Him. Ever since the Fall, a vast chasm separates the God of the Bible and sinful humanity. Do you agree with God's assessment that all human beings, and that includes you too, are fallen sinners?

The only way out: There is *only one* way that leads us out of this dilemma, and this way out was created by God Himself. His Son Jesus Christ fulfilled God's law completely, and for our sakes took the punishment for **all** our sin upon Himself on the Cross. He suffered in our place, and can therefore, in God's name, forgive all who come to Him and want to follow Him. Jesus came to save what is lost (Luke 19:10). Salvation can be found in no-one else and in no other way (Acts 4:12). Do you agree with this fact, too?

Confess your sins: In 1 John 1:8–9 we read: *"If we say we have no sin, we deceive ourselves, and the truth is not in us. If we confess our sins, he is faithful and just to forgive us our sins and to cleanse us from all unrighteousness."*

On the grounds of His saving work on Calvary, Jesus has the authority to forgive sin. If we appeal to His promises and confess our sins to Him, asking Him for forgiveness, you can be sure that He keeps His undertakings. We can depend on it; He will very definitely free us of our burdens and their eternal consequences. Having considered these fundamental issues, now it's a matter of acting upon them. Are you ready for that? If your answer is 'yes', then we can tell the Lord Jesus all that in prayer (what now follows is just a suggestion as the basis for a freely formulated prayer):

"Lord Jesus Christ, up to now I have lived my life as if you did not even exist. Now I want to acknowledge you, and turn to you in prayer. I now know that there is a Heaven, but also a Hell. Please, save me from Hell, from this place that I deserve to go to as a result of all my sins, but most of all for my unbelief. Grant me the right to spend all of eternity with you in Heaven. I understand that I can't get into Heaven through my own efforts, but solely through faith in you. Because you love me, you died for me on the cross and took my sin and guilt upon yourself, and paid for them in my place. I thank you for that from the bottom of my heart. You see all my transgressions, even those from my youth. You know about every sin I have committed; those I remember, but even all those I have long forgotten, too. You know everything about me. Every stirring of my heart is known to you—joy or sadness, delight or despair. Before you, I'm like an open book. Because I cannot stand before you and before God

the Father with my sinful past, access to Heaven is denied to me. That's why I ask you to forgive all my sins, for which I am truly sorry. Amen."

You have now told the Lord everything that is necessary (1 John 1:8–9). God Himself has vouched for this with His promise. What do you think: how much of your guilt is now wiped out? 80 percent? 90 percent? 10 percent? It is written: "*[He] cleanses us from **all** unrighteousness*" (1 John 1:9). You have therefore received **complete** forgiveness! Yes, truly everything, and that is a full 100 percent! If you sincerely meant what you prayed, this is now true for you. The Bible stresses that we should not see the promises of God as somehow imagined, nor as some conceivable possibility or vague hope! For us, it is meant to be a sure and certain fact, and so we read in 1 Peter 1:18–19:

> "**knowing** that you were ransomed … not with perishable things such as silver or gold, but with the precious blood of Christ, like that of a lamb without blemish or spot."

and in 1 John 5:13 the further confirmation:

> "*I write these things to you who believe in the name of the Son of God that **you may know** that you have eternal life.*"

Handing over your life: The Lord Jesus has just now forgiven you all your sin. Now you can trust Him with the whole of your life. In John 1:12 we read: "*But to all* who did receive him, who believed in his name, he gave the right to become children of God." To all who invite the Lord Jesus to take over the rulership of their lives, He gives the right to become children of God. We do not become God's children as a reward for any good deeds, or because of how pious we are, or because we belong to a particular church. We become children of God through His grace, when we entrust our lives to the Son of God and are willing to follow Him obediently, in the power of the Holy Spirit. We want to confirm that, too, in prayer:

> "I receive you now as my Lord and Saviour. May You rule over my life. I want to live a life that is pleasing to you. Please enable me to give up everything that is not right in your eyes, and bless me with new ways of behaving. Help me to understand your Word, the Bible. Help me to understand what you are saying to me, and always to find new joy in your Word. Please show me the way that I should now take, and give me an obedient heart, to follow you. I thank you that you hear my prayer. I believe your promises and thank you that I am now a child of God by your grace, who will one day get to Heaven and spend eternity there. I recognize the amazing benefit of this undeserved grace to me, and I rejoice in the assurance that in every situation of life you will be at my side, even right now. Please help me to find people who also believe in you, and help me to find a church community in which your Word is faithfully preached. Amen."

Accepted: The Lord has accepted you! He has ransomed you at great cost, He has saved you. You have now become a child of God. If you are a child, you are also an heir: an heir of God, an heir of the heavenly world. Can you imagine what is going on right now in Heaven? In Luke 15:10 we read: *"Just so, I tell you, there is joy before the angels of God over one sinner who repents."*

All of Heaven is moved into action whenever someone takes the message of the Gospel seriously and obeys it in their life. The Bible calls this turning to Jesus *conversion*; in this transaction, we give Him our guilt and He removes it. At the same time, God gives us *new birth*: He gives to us the new life of a child of His—we are born again! Now new life has been given to us; we are God's children. Thus *conversion* and *re-birth* belong together—they are two sides of the one coin.

Being thankful: Salvation is God's gift to us. It's only because of His love that this has even become possible. We can contribute absolutely nothing to this deliverance. Anyone who receives something as a gift should say: "Thank you!"—because it's really only when one has returned thanks for something that one has fully accepted it. Why not thank the Lord Jesus now in your own words?

What comes next? The Bible compares your present condition to that of a newborn child. Of course it belongs to its family, and so from now on you belong to the family of God. Newborns find themselves in a critical phase of life. This is also true of our life of faith. Through conversion and new birth everything went well. There is genuine new life. From now on, nourishment (milk) and good care are absolutely essential. Of course God has made provision here too, so that you can experience good development. Damage to our childlike faith can be avoided if we obey God's commandments.

The most powerful sermon that was ever preached on this earth is Jesus' Sermon on the Mount (Matthew 5–7). It opens with the sentence: *"Blessed are the poor in spirit, for theirs is the kingdom of heaven"* (Matthew 5:3). This statement now also applies to you, for you do not as yet know much of the great treasure of the Bible, and feel that you are 'spiritually poor' compared to others who have belonged to Jesus Christ for years, and are following Him. But you have been saved and have gained the entire Kingdom of Heaven. Be aware of this great wealth. As you look for a fellowship of believers, see to it that you do not fall into the clutches of a sect (e.g. Jehovah's Witnesses, Mormons). Try to find a church fellowship in which the teaching is faithful to the Bible and where they emphasise what God has done in history about the sin problem.

The following five aspects are not only meaningful for beginners in the faith, but are indispensable prerequisites for daily living with Jesus. If we take these five points to heart, we fulfil the will of God, and we will also be assured of reaching our designated goal:

1. God's Word

You have based your decision on God's Word, the Bible. The Bible is the only book whose author is God and which is authorized by Him. All the books of the world combined cannot match the Bible as far as truth and quantity of information vital for life are concerned. It is absolutely essential to read and understand the Word of God. In 1 Peter 2:2 this aspect is emphasised and clearly explained: *"Like newborn infants, long for the pure spiritual milk."* Make it a habit to read your Bible daily to discover God's will. It is advisable to begin with the Gospels (e.g. the Gospel of John). There is a certain order to the activities that we run through every morning. On no day do you forget to have breakfast or to brush your teeth. From now on, add the reading of your Bible as a further item to the list of activities you undertake every day.

2. Prayer

From now on, speak with your Lord every day. God speaks to us through His Word. He wants us also to speak with **Him.** It is a great privilege to be able to tell Him everything. According to the Bible, our prayers can only be addressed to God, who is now your Father, and to Jesus, your Saviour, your Good Shepherd, your Friend. The Bible specifically requires that you pray to no-one and nothing else. Any prayer recipients thought up by human beings **and all prayers** not directed to God are idol worship and an abomination to

Him. The Bible testifies to addressing prayer to God the Father and to His Son, Jesus Christ; there is no precedent in the Bible for praying to the Holy Spirit. In prayer you turn to your Lord, who will provide you with strength. This will bring about positive change in your life. Everything in your daily life can become the subject of prayer: your worries, joys and plans. Thank the Lord for everything that moves you. Pray for other people and their difficulties. Pray to the Lord that your family, friends and acquaintances will also come to faith. Prayer and the reading of the divine Word are the pumps for our 'spiritual blood circulation', which in turn is essential for a healthy spiritual life.

3. Obedience

As you read the Bible, you will find many helpful instructions for all areas of your life, including your life in communion with God. Put everything you understand into action and you will experience great blessing. God delights in obedient children, who live according to His Word and keep all His commandments. The best way to show our love to God is to obey Him: *"For this is the love of God, that we keep his commandments"* (1 John 5:3).

The world offers many concepts for living that are drawn from the spirit of the age, which fail in practice. The Bible, on the other hand, points out a way that allows our life to succeed, so that it comes under the blessing of God. With so many choices before us, we decide to follow God's suggestions: *"We must obey God rather than men"* (Acts 5:29). It is important to remember that we are not to satisfy the desires of the old nature, which is called 'the flesh' in this next verse: *"Walk by the Spirit, and you will not gratify the desires of the flesh. For the desires of the flesh are against the Spirit, and the desires of the Spirit are against the flesh, for these are opposed to each other, to keep you from doing the things you want to do"* (Galatians 5:16–17). Because of this, we must make absolutely certain that our obedience toward God is biblically grounded and stands under the power and guidance of the Holy Spirit.

4. Fellowship

God made mankind in order that they might have fellowship with Him and also with one another. Therefore you should look for other Christians who have also submitted their lives to God's directives. These are people with whom you can pray and talk about your faith. Remain in contact with such people, for the members of the congregation are to serve and be a blessing to one another in Jesus Christ (1 Peter 4:10); and where two or three are gathered together in His name, He is there in their midst (Matthew 18:20). If you remove a glowing coal from the fire, it soon grows cold. Just so, our love for Jesus will tend to grow cold if its 'glow' is not maintained in the fellowship of other believers. Join a Bible-believing congregation and take an active part in its fellowship. A good evangelical congregation, where the entire Bible is believed, is of utmost importance for the Christian life. Do not forsake the getting together with those believers for whom it is a priority to rightly understand the Word of God!

5. Maintaining the faith

Our spiritual life began with faith in Jesus' victory on Calvary. Growth is vital for newborns; and it is equally vital that after our conversion and new birth, our spiritual growth is maintained. Paul shows us how in his letter to Timothy: *"But as for you, continue in what you have learned"* (2 Timothy 3:14). At the end of His life, Paul could say: *"I have fought the good fight, I have finished the race, I have kept the faith"* (2 Timothy 4:7). Let us strive to follow this example and also stay faithful!

Read carefully what is written in John 15:4–5 (branches that remain as part of the vine) and Ephesians 4:17–32, containing practical truths about the lifelong sanctification of life in the Spirit.

Conversion is not an end in itself, but rather the beginning of a new life. You are now in a position to be God's fellow worker (1 Corinthians 3:9). Both in your praying and in your witness, strive earnestly for others also to gain the experience of salvation in Jesus. Conversion has two notable consequences: 1) our life on earth becomes truly meaningful, and takes on an entirely new significance; and 2) we become God's children and with that, heirs of eternal life.

Jasmin Yildiz

No Journey Too Far

The fascinating story
of the Ethiopian Treasurer (Acts 8)

In my experience of proclaiming the Gospel I have come to see the story of the Ethiopian Finance Minister (or Treasurer—Acts 8:26–40) as one of the most impressive depictions in the Bible. In it we are introduced to a man searching for God, who, even though he hardly knew anything about God, considered no distance too great, no effort too much and no goal more important than to find eternal life.

Whatever could have moved this high-ranking official to stake everything, all with such consistent determination, on finding the true God? With imaginative freedom, while adhering to the biblical parameters, Jasmin Yildiz has enhanced the story of the Minister, to make it so enthralling that it is impossible to put this booklet down before having read it to the end. Especially for readers who are as yet not familiar with the Bible, this story is a particularly effective aid to understanding the Gospel. In the dialogue between Philip and the Minister, the seeking reader is introduced to the way of salvation in an easy-to-follow manner. Should he then desire to attain eternal life for himself, he will find in the postscript a kind of instruction manual on how to take this vital step to attaining the Kingdom of Heaven.

Werner Gitt, Ph.D.

Bestell-Nr.: 548102   € 1,95